NURSE ABUSE: IMPACT AND RESOLUTION
2nd Edition

Editors
Laura Gasparis Vonfrolio, R.N., Ph.D., CEN, CCRN
Joan Swirsky, R.N., M.S., CS, ACCE
Harold Stearley, R.N., B.S.N., CCRN

I

Library of Congress catalog card number: 90-91915
ISBN 1-888315-02-4

Design and production Coordination: Icon Designs

Printed in the United States of America

Published by

Power Publications
56 McArthur Ave
Staten Island, NY 10312
1-800-331-6534

TABLE OF CONTENTS

PREFACE

Nursing has been practiced in every society throughout history. As long as birthing, living life in both sickness and health, and dying are experiences of the human condition, the need for nursing care will continue to exist.

Today, as health-related concerns have become more complicated, as the AIDS crisis presents the health-care community with challenges and dangers unprecedented in history, as diagnostic techniques have become increasingly sophisticated and treatment regimes more technological, and as the life span has increased in quantum leaps, the need, indeed the demand, for better, smarter, and more empathic health-care has increased as well.

Particularly in the hospital setting, the need for high-level, knowledgeable, and humanitarian nursing care has never before been so urgent. And, because increasing numbers of patients are now being released from hospitals earlier, the need for the same quality of nursing care is now being felt in the home setting as well.

Why, all of sudden, has this need arisen? With more than two-million registered nurses in the United States, what is the problem? The problem, as all hospitals, doctors, patients and nurses know, is that there is a critical shortage of nurses, particularly in our nation's hospitals. So severe has this shortage become that virtually every facet of health-care has been compromised.

Diminishing numbers of staff nurses threaten to deprive patients of the care and attention they have a right to expect. Foreign nurses, recruited from countries in which nursing standards are significantly below our own, now occupy positions of great responsibility. In an attempt to maximize profits, unlicensed assistive personnel have been brought in to replace licensed professionals. And, predicting the even greater problems that will affect the health-care of future generations, the enrollment of nursing schools has started declining precipitously, as it did in the early 1980s.

For some, it appears that shifts in enrollment cannot occur quickly enough. The Pew Health Professionals Commission, in its 1996 report, called for the closure of 10-to-20 percent of all nursing schools in the U.S. Yet another in the list of Nurse Abusers, this commission has joined hospital administrators in an attempt to compromise patient care by staffing hospitals with inferior care providers in the form of unlicensed personnel.

There is some irony here, for never before has the registered-nurse population been better equipped to tend to the public's health-care needs. The modern nurse has both academic and clinical preparation in psychology, pathology, assessment skills, preventive care, as well as knowledge of the social and behavioral sciences. This unique combination of knowledge and expertise enables nurses to assume broad responsibilities in all aspects of health care, including teaching, liaison work, community outreach, and administration.

This versatility has made nursing care essential in the day-to-day operation of major health-care institutions. In fact, nurses are the only professional presence around the clock in both hospitals and nursing homes. The role they play is vital, as their astuteness in clinical assessment, their anticipation of impending crises, and their care-taking capacities are essential to the well-being of all patients. Furthermore, nurses have major responsibilities in managing the operation of the institutions in which they work, in addition to direct accountability for the nursing care they deliver.

Yet in spite of their excellent preparation and society's need for their services, R.N.s are being escorted out of hospital life in ever greater numbers. It is estimated that by the year 2000, we will need an additional 300,000 nurses to meet the needs of our aging population. Despite the staggering increase in need for skilled nursing services, hospital administrators contend they cannot afford to pay for these services. They claim that cost-benefit ratios in health-care have shifted and the maintenance of adequate nurse staffing is not profitable. Omitted is the fact that hospitals routinely pay the high cost of medical complications and malpractice litigation.

In the past, many nurses left hospitals because abusive environments left them suffering from burn out. This phenomenon has been well documented by social scientists, hospital administrators, and nursing academics. Today, however, a shrinking job market has forced nurses to stay in abusive environments and, worse, to face the grave economic threats imposed by rampant lay-offs.

Theoreticians of the past offered numerous studies showing that nurses who experienced "job satisfaction" did not place salary as the primary or most important criterion of employment; they valued working in an environment that allowed them the opportunity to practice in the most effective and compassionate way possible.

But in explaining why so many nurses *did* leave their jobs, some scholars cited the increased opportunity for nurses to work as independent practitioners-as midwives, anesthetists, psycho-therapists, teachers, pediatric specialists, etc. Others mentioned a new "feminist" mentality that inspired women (97 percent of nurses are women) to seek avenues of employment which were more empowering. Other factors included the devalued position of women in society, the disproportionate authority and domi-nance of physicians, and the highly stressful working conditions in hospitals.

Nurses have always had to contend with managers who de-fined, redefined, and stripped away their practice roles. Staff nurses have continually had the latest theories and "Models of Practice" foisted upon them, models which were designed to ex-ploit nurses and, ultimately, drive them away from the practice of nursing.

The latest of these theories is Patient-Focused Care, which operates on the principle of cost-containment and multi-skilling. PFC eliminates registered professional nurses and replaces them with untrained, unlicensed, and unskilled generic health-care workers. Hence, quality of care becomes a secondary issue, and patients suffer or die while nurses stand in unemployment lines.

A number of nurses have sought career opportunities that yield greater economic rewards, and healthier practice environments. But the majority have been blind-sided by the current reduction of skilled nurses in the hospital workforce, caught unaware by administrators' coldly calculated plans to increase profit shares. This abuse of nurses and their patients comes under the guise of "managed care," a euphemism for the greatest *mis*management of care ever to be inflicted on both registered nurses and naively trusting patients.

Many nurses feel powerless to effect changes in their work settings, and resent the inflexibility of their working conditions.

Both society, and especially the tyrannical organizational structure of hospitals, have conditioned nurse to be victims, cowering before authority figures.

The pervasive abuse of nurses permeates our health-care system. It began with the inadequate academic preparation and clinical training nurses received, both devoid of the political realities that drive our system. To this day, it continues in all settings in which nurses work. At times, this abuse has even been promulgated by the very associations and organizations which were designed, originally, to protect nurses in the workplace.

Undervalued, subject to the most ancient and pernicious stereotypes, and treated with cavalier indifference or crass condescension by fellow health professionals, nurses are now beginning to echo the sentiments of the movie hero who, in despair and disgust, exclaimed, "I'm fed up and I'm not going to take it anymore!"

Everyone has their figurative "bottom line," the point past which they cannot be pushed. In the nursing community, the bottom line has been unusually flexible, ever accommodating to the indignities, insults, and shabby treatment which few others would abide. The all-out attack on, and dismantling of, the profession of nursing has now, however, pushed nurses beyond their bottom line. Nurses, too, are beginning to unite and tell the public they will not "take it anymore."

In 1991, when we decided to publish our first volume, *NURSE ABUSE: Impact and Resolution*, nurses responded enthusiastically, happy that, at last, their story would be told. "I'll write it!" some said. "Send me a dozen copies," others exclaimed. "When can I get my hands on a copy — I want to send one to my professor, supervisor, director, attending doctor...." Significantly, not one person asked what the expression **NURSE ABUSE** meant. The note of recognition it inspired was truly amazing.

The intention of writing *NURSE ABUSE: Impact and Resolution, Second Edition*(with Harold Stearley as an additional editor) is twofold: to bring a greater awareness of nursing problems to a public whose needs and interests nurses serve, and to illuminate others who are genuinely interested in resolving this national health emergency — the shortage of registered nurses.

Our authors reviewed their chapters from the book's first edition, adding relevant information and updating their work to make it germane to the 1990s, particularly the past two-or-three years.

It is our hope that this book will act as a catalyst, inspiring our readers to participate in bringing about the long-overdue and meaningful changes that are so urgently needed in the noble profession of nursing.

Laura Gasparis R.N., Ph.D., CEN, CCRN
Joan Swirsky R.N., M.S., CS, ACCE
Harold Stearley, R.N., B.S.N., CCRN

Chapter One

HISTORICAL PERSPECTIVES ON NURSE ABUSE:
HOW IT ALL STARTED

by Susan Giampietro, R.N., M.S., Ph.D.
&
Joy Schloton-Elwell, R.N., M.S.

The word abuse is a painful one, almost shameful. It conjures up images of victims and perpetrators of crimes. It implicates society, and forces awareness of wrong doing. It is accusatory.

Abuse happens, and it happens to the undervalued, and the vulnerable. It happens by them to each other, and to them from within. It is only in recent years that society has permitted abuse to be explored, and more recent still is the notion that abuse is not just physical. Rather, it is multifaceted. *Webster's Dictionary* says that "abuse" means "to put to bad or improper use; to treat without compassion and usually in a hurtful manner; to indicate one's low opinion of something; to take unfair advantage of."

Abuse has a historical dimension, for no society in any epoch has been without it. In nursing, nurses are abused. They have known abuse for the last century and have seen it in all of its definitions. For throughout nursing's long and glorious tradition of service of society runs the covert thread of abuse and nurses' reaction to it — a thread tied to nursing's origins, its mission, and the composition of its labor force.

Nursing's Origins

Modern nursing was born from the abyss of an increasingly industrial society at the height of the Victorian Era. The demise of the Catholic Church in England, and consequently the nursing Sister's orders, had brought an end to any semblance of humanistic care of the sick. Home care was the accepted "system" of health care and its responsibility fell to the women of the family.

Institutional care of the sick was left to criminals, former patients, alcoholics, and prostitutes. Nurses were "generally those who were too old, too weak, too drunken, too dirty, too stolid, or too bad to do anything else" (Nightingale, 1867, p. 274). Care of the sick was not a pressing social issue until the need for it became acute, and was thrust into English consciousness by the insanity of "the greatest organizational mismanagement recorded in history," the Crimean War (Palmer, 1977, p.77).

Enter Florence Nightingale, a member of the privileged class of England, a woman of intellect and education. Nightingale was in search of a meaningful life, committed to returning to society some of the good fortune which was her own lot. Dedicated to social reform at all levels, she had studied nursing in Kaiserwerth, Germany, and obtained a position as superintendent of the Establishment for Gentlewomen During Illness, a charity hospital for governesses.

The outbreak of the Crimean War gave Nightingale an arena in which to practice the ideals of her reform. Singlehandedly, she laid the foundation for the birth of modern nursing, revolutionized the British Army (as well as British society), established the practice of nursing within a military system, legitimized meaningful work for middle-class women outside the home, placed nursing clearly and irrevocably under the authority of the physician, and set the stage for abuse.

While she embodied the definition of a forward-thinking revolutionary, the nursing model Nightingale introduced was a product of its time. Although she was a political-science genius, and her love of and commitment to nursing were evidenced in the way she led her life, that commitment was secondary to her desire for social reform. Her goal was success and her methods set the stage for the respectability of nursing, as well as its feminization, but they also set the stage for nursing's subservience, its social-class distinction, and its educational system.

In accordance with the prevailing attitude of Victorianism, Nightingale believed that women possessed moral superiority and were, therefore, uniquely suited to the work of social reform. Consequently, women were believed to be better suited to nursing than men: "Their innate sensitivity would bring warmth and reassurance to the patient, as it brought cleanliness and order to the ward" (Rosenberg, 1987, p. 217).

In America too, where health-care reform was still in its infancy, nursing was believed to belong to the special domain of women. "Nursing is as absolutely the peculiar province of women as any branch of house-wifery. The qualities of a good nurse are vigilance, discretion, and gentleness; and these are her special qualities" (Smith, 1862, p. 149). In keeping with this attitude, Nightingale selected only women to accompany her to Scutari. Hence, nurses were and continue to be, for the most part, women.

Moral superiority and unique skills notwithstanding, women were indeed women, and relegated to second-class status in society. They were not welcomed into the unique domain of men, especially in that most masculine of traditions, the military. Nightingale was well aware of this problem, and when drafting the terms of her commission, she placed nursing "clearly and unequivocally under medical and administrative authority" (Palmer, 1983, p. 4). She knew her mission would be a failure, should any other method for the organization of nurses be suggested.

But in spite of her concessions to the Victorian mentality concerning women and nursing, Nightingale waged a constant battle. Organized nursing's first assignment, while sanctioned by the British people, was met with abuse at the hands of the male military. Nurses were not wanted, their services were not valued. Simply, they were women in a man's world. It was here that nursing's relationship to the masculine medical and hospital behaviors of rejection, resistance, and scorn was first established.

Of great importance to the status of nursing was the social class from which Nightingale came. An aristocrat, she never viewed the nurse as her equal, believing that the only role for "ladies" in a hospital was that of hospital matron. Even after nurses had received their training, Nightingale viewed them as belonging to the servant class. "She established hours of work comparable to those of servants in English households and recommended similar living conditions: small rooms with plain, simple furniture" (Palmer, 1983, p. 6). Thus, the concept of nursing as a blue-collar occupation was born.

Possibly as an outgrowth of her belief that nurses occupied the servant class, Nightingale did not establish a tradition of university-based nursing education, even while adamantly espousing the philosophy that nurses must know the "why" of all of their actions. However, Nightingale *did* bring reforms to nursing education; prior to her efforts, there had been none.

But she remained firmly convinced that the hospital should be where nurses were trained and she never wavered from this belief. (While nursing education did not enter the halls of universities during Nightingale's lifetime, she was also fierce in her belief that the training schools be separate from hospital administration and from the regulation of the hospital itself. Nightingale schools were not run by hospital administrators or physicians).

Nightingale never crossed the Atlantic, but the stories of her success and methods did. Unfortunately, along with her triumphs, came the seeds of nursing's abuse as an occupation of middle-class, apprenticeship-trained women.

Nursing's Mission

The service which society expects of nursing is care. At a time when curing was rare, and industrial society could no longer count on the female members of the family to provide caring services in their entirety, nursing was born. It was born out of society's need for a group of individuals to assume responsibility for the care of the sick. While nurses and nursing were initially met with great social respect and gratitude, those feelings waned as society got on with more pressing issues.

Reverby (1987, p. 1) posits that nursing's dilemma stems from "...the order to care in a society that refuses to value caring." Historically the mission of nursing, caring, gained attention only when caring needs were acute. In both the United States and Britain, the need for organized care of the sick was not recognized until the outbreak of war. The tragedy of the hospital system that existed prior to these events was not enough to spur reform. Training schools for nurses were founded in the decade following the Civil War, and a respected occupation for women arose.

As nursing was organized and the ranks of nurses swelled, the profession enjoyed relative importance in the health-care arena. Nurses were "Angels of Mercy," women with a divine calling. Each American war improved the social image of nurses. The Spanish-American War saw the first organized Army Nurse Corps in U.S. history, and underscored the need for caring during times of great social strife. Nurses, through caring, not fighting, died serving their country, and battled disease through participation in scientific research. The influenza epidemic and both World Wars again forced society to value the service nursing provided. Perhaps if the Great

Depression of 1929 had not occurred, nurses would have enjoyed the continued growth in status that appeared to have been developing until that point in history.

In 1920, 70-to-80 percent of all nurses worked in private duty, practicing independently and autonomously. Contracting their services through registries, they selected assignments in patients' homes or chose private-duty cases in the hospital setting. While the nursing literature of the day is replete with stories of economic instability, deference to "social superiors," and long, arduous work days, nurses escaped the rigid demands imposed by institutional work. They were, indeed, their own bosses.

"As freelance workers, nurses could schedule cases to suit their own needs and preferences. They could take time off to rest after a tiring stint, or take themselves off the registrar's list temporarily if sick friends or relatives needed their help. Freelance arrangements also gave nurses the opportunity to evade unappealing work situations, a prerogative they exercised freely. Private-duty nurses constantly thwarted the registrars' efforts to impose discipline and order by picking and choosing among cases the registrar offered. Doctors, nursing leaders, and registrars complained bitterly about that practice. [Nurses] routinely refused certain types of cases, boldly listing their restrictions with the registrar...a nurse could declare herself `off duty' if confronted with an unappealing prospect" (Melosh, 1982, p. 80).

Nurses' power to control their practice can be seen in the action taken by Chicago nurses who were registered with the West Suburban Hospital during this early 20th Century era. To the satisfaction of themselves and their patients, these nurses were working 12-hour shifts. The medical board, apparently resentful of the nurses' satisfaction and control, influenced the hospital's administration to enforce a policy requiring that, "...any nurse registering with the hospital accept $6.00 for a 12-hour assignment or $7.00 for a 24-hour assignment, and further, that she must be willing to accept any type of service for which she was called" (Nurses Strike, 1927, p. 34).

The nurses found this unacceptable, for themselves as well as their patients, and sought legal counsel. Acting upon their lawyers' advice, they refused to leave their patients, but, when the case was complete, the nurses declined future cases at the hospital. Panicking, the hospital's administration responded by publicizing their actions as a "strike," when, in fact, the nurses were simply opting to decline further services.

Both the rise of the hospital industry and the economic impact of the Depression on the health-care consumer adversely affected the autonomy of the freelance nurse. The public was increasingly unable to afford the service of private-duty nursing, and functioning in an entrepreneurial fashion became impossible. Nurses found themselves in dire financial situations, and turned to their alma maters for assistance. As a result, they became dependent on the hospital structure for their very lives, many offering their services in exchange for food and lodging.

As employees, nurses found themselves under the control and domination of a male medical and administrative hierarchy. Even as nursing leaders sought to protect nurses and the public with licensure, nurses were suffering the abuse of second-class status within a masculine, medically oriented health-care system.

While nurses enjoyed relative social appreciation during World War II (again, a time during which caring needs were acutely felt by the public), they were not given equal status either in commission or salary during their military service because of their gender. After the war, when most women returned to their roles in the private sector to "make room for their returning men," the image of nursing took a nose-dive. It was during the post-War period that the image of nurses as loose women and prostitutes gained popularity, a dramatic change from the Angels of Mercy image of the war years.

Nursing's Ranks

Perhaps the most fertile field for NURSE ABUSE exists because of the fact that nursing's ranks are, and always have been, comprised predominantly of women. "Barriers created by restrictive and oppressive social ideologies about women have served to retard the growth of nursing as a profession and to limit the full development of nursing's potential" (Kalish, 1978, p. 139). Nursing has long been viewed as a natural extension of the innate abilities or women, and, as a consequence, has always been considered "women's work." This myth has set the stage for a history of abusive educational and service practices.

Schools of nursing arose in the United States in response to the cries of wealthy women who recognized the need for organized caregiving in hospitals. Unfortunately, unlike in the United Kingdom, financial support for the training of nurses was not forthcoming. The education of nurses was not, in and of itself, high on the agenda of hospitals of the day; submissive, compliant, and available personnel were. This was the framework from which hospital-based nursing education originated.

Cloaked under the guise of altruism, women entered nurses' "training," which, in actuality, more closely resembled hard labor. Consistent with the philosophy of the time, real education occurred sporadically. Since it was believed that all women were born with an innate ability to nurse, teaching them to do "what comes naturally" was considered a wasted effort. What nurses *did* need to learn was humility, subservience to physicians, and their place in the institution. Nursing education was really considered character development, and a refinement of the socially accepted place of the woman. Nursing admission criteria reflected this.

When nursing schools arose in the U.S., admission requirements deemed that applicants be between the ages of 25 and 35, single or widowed, and in a state of "good health." The life of the student nurse was dominated by 12-hour days on the ward. Lectures were sporadic, and coincidental to the real work of the institution, patient care. Student nurses scrubbed floors, rolled bandages, and prepared and delivered food. They were granted a half day of leisure per week, and one day off to attend religious services. In her book, *Ordered to Care*, Susan Reverby describes the magnitude of the abuse:

"The danger of typhoid and scarlet fever, pneumonia, and diphtheria could be measured in the high morbidity and mortality rates among students. Tuberculosis felled or permanently disabled many. Under the pressure of work, students were often required to return to service before they were completely recovered. Sick leaves were rare, and 'exhaustion' was the leading reason for student withdrawals. Poor living conditions compounded the problem, as nursing quarters were more barracks than homes" (Reverby, 1987, p. 64).

Women were not valued, the work of women was not valued, and education of women for the work of caring was not valued. Rather than educate women, nursing education provided the patriarchal medical-care system with a virtually free, never-ending supply of supplicant workers. But abuse did not end with educational content. Hospital administrations were well aware that placing nursing education under the independent control of nurses would result in chaos, and the possible demise of the system as they knew it. As hospital hierarchies evolved, it was determined by physicians and hospital administrators alike that nursing remain under their control, not only to assure unity, but for the good of the hospital "family" as well.

Attempts to educate women to become nurses in a collegiate setting opened the doors for further abuse, as nurses provided willing, albeit unknowing, complicity in their continuing downward spiral to a lower-status occupation. In an effort to operationalize the suggestions of the Goldmark and Brown reports of 1948, which strongly recommended, among other things, that nursing education take place in institutions of higher learning, nursing leaders took action to revise and upgrade educational standards. This attempt was met with great opposition from nursing's rank and file.

Nurses identified strongly with their alma maters and clung tenaciously to their educational system. Nurses themselves, so indoctrinated into a social system which valued the practical over the theoretical base for nursing, believed that too much education for nurses was not only unnecessary, but dangerous, and would produce a generation of nurses who "would not want to dirty their hands with the real stuff of nursing." If nursing is a natural extension of femininity, these nurses believed, why should women be educated to do it?

Furthermore, any kind of education for women was actually believed to be detrimental to a woman's health and family. Into the chaos of educational reform came the devastating, and counter-productive, introduction of yet another method of nursing education, the Associate Degree Registered Nurse. Without ever resolving the issue of a single appropriate method of nursing preparation, community colleges began offering a two-year curriculum for nursing education in the 1950s. At a time when women in general were suffering great setbacks in economic and social issues, this was not surprising. With the end of World War II, those women who had been welcomed into the workplace were now being shown the door back to their homes. In order to fit the social expectation of the day, they were to marry and take care of hearth, home, and children.

Any education for a woman was simply to provide her with temporary entertainment prior to her assuming her true role, that of wife and mother. It is an indictment of nursing's leaders of the day that greater foresight was not demonstrated in deciding how these programs were to be utilized. For a profession to take a step backward in the amount of education required for entry set an historical precedent. For nursing to have suggested, or agreed to, an educational preparation of two years versus three (albeit that education in a collegiate setting), was, in hindsight, disastrous for the status of the profession.

It set the stage for the further abuse of nurses, as men and women, educated to be "technical" nurses, were utilized in practice, side by side with nurses educated for a "professional" role. While the intent may have been the creation of two levels of caregiver, the reality was a cheaper and less-well-educated product. Nurses abused nursing, hospitals abused the nurses, and the stage was set for the scorn of the public.

Nursing's Challenge

In her analysis of society's patriarchal system, Gerda Lerner (1986) is careful to point out that while women have been subordinate to men throughout history, they did not play the role of submissive victim. The same is true of nurses. Many took radical action against their subordination and many enjoyed relatively autonomous status within the health-care system. And nurses were at the forefront of the suffrage movement early in this century. But nurses are, and have been, women who do "women's work" in a world where women and their work are of questionable value. This is still true, despite the fairly recent entry of males into the profession, who now comprise approximately three-to-five percent of R.N.s.

Our entire society is designed to overlook and devalue nurturing and caring, for it is based upon a patriarchal paradigm. The ideals of achievement and aggression, so totally unnecessary and unrelated to nursing's mission, are the stuff of "success" in modern society. All people in a society learn to hold in contempt those who are not valued. For at least the past two centuries, women, and consequently nurses, have filled the bill.

What once was can no longer be. History cannot be rewritten, nor its value system changed. However, that which has not served humankind well can be re-thought. The exclusively masculine paradigm within which we have lived and operated, that world view which devalues more than half of society's members, and in so doing robs us all, must no longer be accepted. Then, nurses will find a place of worth in society. Then, nurses will no longer find or allow themselves to be the recipients of NURSE ABUSE.

Postscript by Harold Stearley

Over the past two decades, the enrollment of men in professional nursing has been on the rise. The profession is now comprised of 97 percent women and three percent men. Men began entering the profession faster during the nursing shortage of the 1980s, as wages and benefits improved to the point they could support their families.

When men entered nursing, many female nurses believed those men would attempt to dominate and control the profession. Others believed that if males elevated nursing's status, they would again be playing a secondary, "helpless" role. Still more commentary raged around the topic of incompetence: "These males, like their female counterparts, must have been too stupid to become doctors!" And, since social stereotypes go both ways, many people could not imagine that males would be capable of giving compassionate care.

Some of these were understandable concerns. Women have worked long and hard at elevating the nursing profession and they didn't want males "messing things up." But, by becoming nurses, males, including myself, have gained great understanding of the ABUSE women have been subjected to for centuries. After all, we are now subjected to the same abuses, the imperiousness of doctors, for one.

For instance, I am expected to handle patient problems by myself so as not to disturb physicians, while my female counter-parts, their judgment always doubted, are told to report the tiniest detail to doctors. The message: if I report an incident, I am stupid; if a female nurse does not report an incident, she is stupid!

For both the females and males who choose it, nursing is a noble profession requiring intelligence, skill, inventiveness, compassion, humor and the ability to survive NURSE ABUSE! It will be interesting to see how the history of our profession evolves and what "new chapters" may be written in the future.

References

Kalisch, P.A. and Kalisch, B.J. (1978). *The Advance of American Nursing*. Boston: Little, Brown and Company.

Lerner, G. (1986). *The Creation of Patriarchy*. New York: Oxford University Press.

Melosh, B. (1982). *The Physician's Hand: Work, Culture, and Conflict in American Nursing*. Philadelphia: Temple University Press.

Nightingale, F. (1867). "Suggestions on the subject of providing training and organizing nurses for the sick poor in workhouse infirmaries." Reprinted in Lucy R. Seymer, *Selected Writings of Florence Nightingale*. New York: Macmillan.

"Nurses Strike?" (January, 1927). *American Journal of Nursing*.

Palmer, I.S. (1977). Florence Nightingale: Reformer, reactionary, researcher. Reprinted from *Nursing Research*, March/April, in Pages From Nursing History, A collection of Original Articles for the Pages of Nursing Outlook, *The American Journal of Nursing* and *Nursing Research*. (1984). New York: American Journal of Nursing Company.

Palmer, I.S. (1983). Nightingale revisited. Reprinted from *Nursing Outlook*, July/August, in Pages From Nursing History, A Collection of Original Articles for the Pages of Nursing Outlook, *The American Journal of Nursing* and *Nursing Research*. (1984). New York: American Journal of Nursing Company.

Reverby, S. (1987). *Ordered to Care: The Dilemma of American Nursing, 1850-1945*. New York: Cambridge University Press.

Rosenberg, C.E. (1987). *The Care of Strangers: The Rise of America's Hospital System*. New York: Basic Books, Inc.

Smith, S. (September 13, 1862). Female nurses in hospitals. *American Medical Times*.

Chapter Two

DESENSITIZATION TO NURSE ABUSE

by Harold Stearley, R.N., B.S.N., CCRN

The life-threatening diseases, caustic chemicals, carcinogenic drugs, radiation, and mechanical and electrical hazards nurses face daily in their work environments pale in comparison to the physical and mental abuse to which they are relentlessly subjected. Numerous studies document that, everyday, nurses risk being assaulted by criminals, patients, patients' family members, the physicians with whom they practice, and the managers who direct them.

Nurses are assaulted in patients' rooms, in emergency rooms, in hospital corridors, and in hospital parking lots. They are besieged in staffing offices, administrative committees, and during physicians' rounds. Nurses are even battered by their own nursing leaders. For instance, the American Nurses Association's policy statements offer guidelines which, de facto, sanction the mistreatment of nurses. This abuse has become so commonplace, so ingrained in our health-care-delivery system, that it has become standard accepted practice.

Physical Abuse in the Workplace

The Bureau of Justice reports one-million violent crimes occur in the workplace annually. Eight percent of all rapes, seven percent of all robberies, and 16 percent of all assaults occur under the supervision, or non-supervision, of employers. Women are most frequently victimized, while 85 percent of the time, the perpetrator is a young male (Staff , 1995 - 2, p. 14).

By and large, the overwhelming majority of nurses (97 percent) are female. In addition to their gender placing them at "ground zero," their choice of occupation appears to have doubled their exposure to violence. Many studies reveal that nurses work in a battle zone of physical and psychological violence.

Whether the assault is verbal, physical, or committed with a weapon, the fact remains that nurses are abused at an alarming rate and the numbers are rising. It takes only one assault to leave a person irreparably injured, either mentally, physically, or both.

In a recent survey of emergency department nurses, 97 percent said they were verbally abused more than 20 times a year, 87 percent were assaulted without weapons at least five times a year, and 24 percent were assaulted with weapons one-to-five times a year. A startling 67 percent of the staff said they experienced emotional injuries! (Staff, 1995 - 2, p. 14).

It would *seem* only logical that hospital management would be supportive of its staff nurses and take whatever measures necessary to protect them from abusive environments. After all, it is the nurse who provides direct, hands-on care for patients who are the hospital's source of revenue. In reality, such support costs money and cuts profits.

It costs money to hire security guards and pay greater insurance premiums to arm those guards so, should a crime occur, they are capable of taking action. Only 78 percent of hospital emergency rooms employ uniformed security guards, and only 18 percent of these guards are allowed to carry weapons (Staff, 1995 - 2, p. 14).

In some hospitals, crimes are perpetrated so frequently that seven percent now staff off-duty police officers, but only 72 percent of these officers can arrest or detain suspects (Staff, 1995 - 2, p. 14). How many crimes have to be committed, and how many nurses must be injured or killed, to make it economically practical for managers to protect their staffs?

Recently, a security guard at my hospital told me in confidence that "someone will have to be killed before management takes any action." He also informed me that he and his colleagues were prohibited from securing the building, not only because of prohibitive costs, but because the "image" of locking a healing institution at night was "bad p.r. for the hospital."

The guard went on to tell me, somewhat apologetically, that he was sorry the hospital didn't allow him to carry a weapon. "There would be little I could do to protect the nurses without one," he said. He explained that it was too costly to buy each security guard a $400-dollar protective vest "to prevent the guards from being shot." Ironically, this managerial dictate came on a day the institution had budgeted over $100 million in capital improvements — a day following a crime in which a local policeman's life had been saved by having worn a bullet-proof vest!

When hospitals use security cameras, they are commonly limited in number and placed to monitor the most frequently trafficked areas of the hospital, not the dark recesses of the building which are the choice areas for criminals to commit their assaults. Again, it costs money to place cameras throughout an institution and hire people to monitor them. And it's cheaper to look at films of entrances and exits *after* someone has already been victimized to try to identify the perpetrator. Management then apologizes, and denies any liability.

Physician Abuse of Nurses

When it comes to security, no employee of the hospital will intervene if a physician is abusing a nurse. Doctors can essentially do whatever they want to, because they are the gatekeepers of medical dollars. Strike a nurse, sexually assault or harass a nurse, scream at and brow-beat a nurse, terrorize and threaten a nurse— it's all fair game if you're licensed to practice medicine.

Often, physicians will not tolerate nurses who make suggestions regarding patient care. No idea, which is not theirs, is welcome. Yet nurses are charged with the responsibility of challenging any orders which are incorrect, or which pose a danger to their patients.

How many times a day do nurses find themselves attempting, tactfully, to get a doctor to change his or her orders, or to order what is appropriate, only to be screamed at, insulted, struck, or worse? And, how many times do physicians take credit for nurses' ideas, or return hours later to order what a nurse has suggested, acting as though it was he or she who originated the idea?

If a nurse complains to management about a physician's behavior, s/he can count on her grievance being dismissed with little or no action being taken. If nurses persist in complaining, management's usual course of action is to discipline the complaining nurse, deny the existence of any problem, and treat the nurse as if s/he is the problem!

When Meryl Szczepanski, R.N., was physically assaulted by a physician at Newcomb Hospital in New Jersey, management's response was totally predictable. They fired her for reporting the sexual assault and battery, and fabricated a long list of lies about her performance to justify their own criminal actions (Tammelleo, 1995, p. 1).

Ultimately, they paid a price for their actions in court, but Nurse Szczepanski paid a much greater price in terms of the emotional damage inflicted on her, not just from the assault, but from the total abandonment of her employer. This type of incident occurs daily, but most are not reported because the majority of nurses fear such heartless retaliation.

Physical and Mental Abuse in a Hazardous Work Environment

Nurse managers abuse their staffs every time they refuse to provide adequate coverage for nurses to take care of their patients. Staff nurses are stretched to the limit attempting to provide some semblance of quality care. When there is one R.N. for 20 patients or one R.N. for four ventilated, intensive-care-unit patients, administrative abuse is clearly evident. Nurses working under these conditions must make daily decisions about which patients will or will not receive the superior care they deserve, and which patients will not even receive adequate care.

Nurses abused in this fashion run from crisis to crisis. Should a lawsuit evolve from a patient receiving poor nursing intervention, nurses cannot, and should not, believe their administration will stand behind them. In most cases, nursing management is unconcerned if nurses lose their licenses. Rather, they are concerned about their own liability and the bad publicity they might receive from being exposed.

The Patient-Focused Care model is management's most recent attempt to bury nurses. This "model" follows years of others that were also designed to exploit nurses and maximize hospital profits. At the same time hospitals are understaffing nurses and taking more dollars away from patient services, they are purchasing elaborate computer programs called "Patient Classifications Systems" or "Acuity/Staff Measurement Tools."

Using a list of indicators, these systems are designed for nursing staff to estimate the number of hours of nursing care required for patients on individual units. This value is then magically converted into the number of nurses, and the staffing mix, required to provide patient care. Each patient is given a classification according to his or her acuity level, which is then used to determine the individual nurse's assignment.

The problems with such systems become obvious upon closer examination. When I attended a seminar on my hospital's PCS to learn what was in store for the nursing staff, I was shocked to realize that the system didn't factor any time for nurses to perform any type of assessment on their patients! There were no indicators to measure the time required to review a patient's pertinent medical history; to review medication, proper dosage, or the prevention of an adverse drug reaction; to interpret complex monitoring systems; to evaluate the effectiveness of nursing interventions; or to monitor the interventions of other members of the health-care team, such as physical, respiratory, or occupational therapists. No time was allowed for attending to patients' social, emotional, or spiritual needs, or to obtain necessary supplies.

When I asked the programmers how they converted "measured acuities" into patient-care hours and staffing needs, I was told it depended on the things the institution had "front-loaded" into their system. In other words, the conversion factor was totally arbitrary and subject to the whim of management, designed, in even high acuity cases, to kick out low numbers of nurses required to care for gravely ill patients.

To prevent what the representative referred to as "acuity creeping" which results when R.N.s, realize they are being exploited the programmers had built in a security system that allowed management to track and discipline nurses. The security systems are designed to prevent staff from obtaining the information used to make the conversions and the actual dollar calculations, insuring management's ability to manipulate staffing to arrive at a specific dollar-per-day patient cost!

Of course, the PCS representatives claimed the system was 92-95 percent accurate in converting actual patient needs into nurse staffing. How did they validate their claims? "Studies," they said.

Could I obtain any research information that validated the effectiveness of such systems? "No."

In essence, the institution maintains it is providing adequate staffing while, in fact, it simply creates artificial numbers designed to justify its deliberate understaffing— yet another form of NURSE ABUSE.

In addition to providing fewer nurses for a patient population of increasing age and acuity, nurse managers are now decreasing the orientation time for graduating nurses. The graduate nurse may now receive only one week of orientation to a medical-surgical floor, and three weeks to an intensive-care unit. And, yes, hospitals are now hiring graduate nurses straight into ICUs with no experience whatsoever, which allows the hospital to cut down the cost of hiring more experienced nurses.

Reducing the quantity and experience levels of hospital nurses is, in itself, a major detriment to the provision of safe patient care. Another detriment is forcing new graduates to delegate and supervise the care provided by an ever-increasing number of nursing assistants who have had *no* experience and minimal training — some as little as three to 12 weeks! How, then can nurses be expected to perform in such abusive environments?

With nursing staffs decreasing, workplace injuries are dramatically rising. In one Minnesota study, it was noted that as the R.N.s in the local bargaining units decreased by nine percent, injuries for the remaining nurses increased from 6.35 percent to 11.75 percent! (Himali, 1995, p. 19.) Nurses who had to lift, turn, and ambulate patients by themselves experienced increased morbidity and mortality of both patients (who weren't moved properly), and nurses (who injured their backs).

It is clear that management prefers paying the lower costs of workman's compensation claims than providing adequate nursing staff to meet patients' needs. One research study (*Circulation*) revealed that nurses working rotating shifts for six or more years had a 50-to-70 percent increase in risk for myocardial infarction (Kawachi, 1995, p. 3178), a risk that remained for years after discontinuing shift work.

Why should nurses be subjected to such drastic changes in schedules? Why not consolidate shift work and space working days to reduce the stress levels and physical toll extracted by such labor practices? Management defends its practices by claiming it pays "shift differentials," again demonstrating total disregard for the health and well-being of its health-care providers.

Management again demonstrates its disregard when it comes to the mental anguish nurses experience. Unable to care properly for their patients, nurses internalize their patient's suffering, often going home in tears because they were unable to make a difference or prevent complications, or because they witnessed another death without receiving much-needed support. When will nurses reach the point when they have run out of tears?

Nurse Abuse by Organizations and Associations

Even the American Nurses Association has contributed to the abuse of nurses. Their representatives maintain their policies have been misused, but they cannot deny they created guidelines for the use of unlicensed assistive personnel in their position statement, "Registered Nurse Utilization of Unlicensed Assistive Personnel" (December 11, 1992), and its associated attachments.

These guidelines are now mounted in hospital corridors throughout the country, corridors filled with unlicensed assistants. In today's hospital, one must search hard to find an R.N.; hence, more and more R.N.s are turning away from organized nursing and its domination by nursing managers and academics.

The ANA had captured the membership of 10 percent of this nation's 2.2 million nurses, before, that is, 10 percent of their membership from the California Nurses Association decided to secede in 1995. Refusing to admit they lost this important group of nurses, the ANA continues to let corporate dollars and membership dues drive their agenda. Staff nurses are still waiting for the calvary to arrive, but it appears it won't be on the ANA's horses.

In fact, the ANA has never allowed staff nurses, which comprise 75 percent of their membership, to have meaningful participation in the determination of their policies and positions. The ANA's House of Delegates, which votes on such decisions, is comprised of nursing administrators and academics; 76 percent of the HOD's votes are controlled by the very people who fabricate the nursing-care-delivery models and nurse-staffing ratios that *exclude* R.N.s from the workforce (Bayer & Kuhl, 1995, p.3).

Instead of drafting position statements opposing the use of Unlicensed assistance personnel (UAP), the ANA has adopted disciplinary measures for any state association that opposes their dictates. Instead of using their $21-million-dollar budget to educate the public with their own program, "Every Patient Deserves a Nurse," the ANA has asked staff nurses who are clinging to limited jobs with poor wages to *buy* their brochures and distribute them (*Staff*, 1995, p. 8).

And instead of rewarding and honoring staff nurses for joining the struggle to prevent the layoffs of R.N.s, the American Nurses Foundation of the ANA awarded Connie Curran the "First Distinguished Scholar in Residence" award. Ms. Curran is a top official of American Practice Management, a consulting firm that specializes in reorganizing health institutions to lay off registered nurses (*Staff*, 1994, p. 4).

Nurse Abuse in the Home Perpetuated by Health-Care Insurers

Nurses, predominately women, not only face the possibility of assault at their workplaces, but from their own spouses or partners. One out of every 20 women surveyed had experienced physical or mental abuse in her own home in 1995. One out of every five had experienced physical violence during her adult life, and one out of every three women reported being victimized during her lifetime! (McCauley, 1995, p. 737.)

Mental and physical abuse of women has become so accepted, so rampantly carried out by perpetrators, and so purposely ignored by legal and legislative bodies, it is tantamount to a national scandal. Most abusers deny the abuse, just as batterers deny they have beaten someone within an inch of their lives. Because of this denial, the overt acts of violence inflicted upon women have actually increased, while our society, wishing to call itself morally superior, refuses to open its eyes to its own social pathology.

We stand at the brink of another century, calling ourselves the most advanced species on the planet, while half of the world's population faces the prospect of being murdered by someone they have chosen as their partner. More murders are committed in this country every year by spouses than by any other demographic group; thus, the new terminology to describe this form of terror — "domestic violence."

While we count the bodies, does our society strive to eliminate this problem? Unfortunately not. Rather, it does more to trap women in these situations than to help them escape. If this is not sad enough, abused nurses now face another nemesis: health-insurance companies that deny them coverage *because* they are victimized women. Yes, health-care insurers have become yet another link in the chain of violence perpetrated against women.

Among the current wave of cutting coverage to "high-risk" patients in order to maximize insurance profits, insurance companies deny coverage to victims of domestic violence, deeming them to be living "high-risk lifestyles." A single beating is now a "pre-existing condition." Only five states have passed laws to eliminate this type of discrimination—five out of fifty! (Rovner, 1995, p. 690.)

How long will it be before being a nurse will be classified as a "high risk lifestyle"? With the many dangers and risks nurses face daily, there is no question it is perilous to become a nurse. How long will it be before all of our nation's hospitals abandon their primary caretakers altogether?

The Battering Syndrome

The behavior patterns women develop in response to being continually victimized—significant increases in anxiety, depression, somatization, and low self-esteem—now have an official title: "The Battering Syndrome." Low self-esteem permeates the nursing profession. Nurses have been treated with such disrespect for so long, they have come to disrespect themselves.

After being kicked around again and again by managers, physicians, occasionally their patients, and even their spouses, nurses understandably begin to question their own self-worth. They wonder if they are performing a quality job, they blame themselves for everything, and they navigate their work environments with their heads bowed, ashamed to stand up for their rights. This is exactly where those in power want nurses to be: totally demoralized and, therefore, easy to manipulate.

From childhood to adulthood, we are all taught to work hard and be truthful and loyal. For nurses, who take it for granted that others learn the same lessons, it comes as a shock to realize that some of these "others" are abusive and exploitive. Time and time again, I hear nurses making excuses for the same managers who have just victimized them!

When Will the Abuse End?

Abuse upon abuse upon abuse. It's a wonder there are any people left in this country who want to become nurses! Of course, the new Patient-Focused Care models have reinforced management's desire to eliminate nurses anyway. In their view, a janitor can provide nursing care.

Nevertheless, there are untold numbers of highly motivated people who still believe that caring for others is a noble calling. Unfortunately, the abuse of nurses continues to be widespread and blatant. In essence, nurses have become desensitized to it and accept it as sort of a hazing ritual that is required of anyone who wants to join the professional ranks of the staff nurse.

What is the solution? Nurses must acknowledge the presence of abuse and exploitation and fight back. Only when denial ends and a take-charge mentality prevails will nurses be able to take control of their profession, and reclaim their self-respect.

References

American Nurses Association (1993). Policy: ANA Intervention in Cases of Threats to Nursing Practice. *Responsibilities of ANA Board of Directors*, Effective Date: April 2, 1993.

Bayer, D. & Kuhl, M. (1995). Report from ANA House of Delegates. *California Nurse*, 91(7), 3.

Himali, U. (1995). An Unsafe Equation: Fewer R.N.s Equals More Workplace Injuries. *The American Nurse*, 27(5), 19.

Kawachi, I., et al. (1995). Prospective Study of Shift Work and Risk of Coronary Heart Disease in Women. *Circulation*, 92(11), 3178-3182.

McCauley, J., et al. (1995). The Battering Syndrome: Prevalence and Clinical Characteristics of Domestic Violence in Primary Care Internal Medicine Practices. *Annals of Internal Medicine*, 123(10), 737-746.

Rovner, J. (1995). Insurance Discrimination for Domestic Violence Victims. *The Lancet*, 346, 690.

Staff. (1994). ANF Linked to Health Care Management. *California Nurse*, 90(10), 4.

Staff. (1995). Staff Nurses Take Action Against Unsafe Care: Every R.N. Asked to Distribute 250 Consumer Brochures. *The American Nurse*, 27(5), 8.

Staff. (1995 -2). ENA Survey Examines Facets of Workplace Violence. *The American Nurse*, 27(6), 14.

Tammelleo, D. A. (ed.) (1995). Nurse Reports Sexual assault by Doctor: Retaliatory Termination. *The Regan Report on Nursing Law*, 36(5), 1.

Chapter Three

COMMON FORMS OF NURSE ABUSE

by Donna Shea Leear, R.N., B.S.N., CCRN
&
Cathy Odorisio, R.N., B.S.N., MSN

The trials and tribulations in the lives of student nurses place them in the fast lane of one of the most significant components of NURSE ABUSE—professional abuse. After discussing the many abuses to which student nurses are exposed, we will elaborate upon professional abuse, which can be subdivided into several categories: 1) Nurse-to-Nurse Abuse, 2) Physician-to-Nurse Abuse, 3) Administration-to-Nurse Abuse, 4) Environment-to-Nurse Abuse, and 5) Financial Abuse. We will also discuss Media Abuse of nurses.

It's 11 p.m. You are the charge nurse for the midnight-to-7:00 a.m. shift in a 10-bed medical-surgical intensive-care unit. Conscientious and dedicated, you always arrive "just a few minutes early" for your shift. After depositing your belongings, you leave the locker room and head for the unit. As you walk to the nurses' station through the electric doors, you note that the area is astir with activity.

Right on your heels is a patient being transferred to the ICU from the emergency department. A code blue, or patient having a cardiac arrest, is taking place in bed seven. The phone is ringing off the hook; it's the laboratory calling with blood-analysis results. The admitting office is calling to find out the correct patient census. The family of the patient who has just been admitted to the unit is calling to find out his status.

More and more frequently, the scenario being played out before your eyes is the norm for your shift. The charge nurse from the previous shift is tugging at your arm, ready to start report, albeit 15 minutes early, because she has "had enough" and wants to go home on time. She tells you that there was supposed to be four nurses booked for your shift, but one nurse called in sick.

At the same time, the recovery room has called to say that you're getting a patient—but you have no bed available. The emergency-department nurse is yelling in the middle of the nurse's station for someone to listen to her report, and the ICU physician, rather belligerent, says he needs someone to assist him for a pulmonary-artery-line insertion (a large catheter inserted into the venous system and through the heart to make diagnostic determination for therapeutic treatments) for the patient in Bed Four.

You call your nursing supervisor to obtain assistance, but you're told she is not available, that you will have to "make do" with what you have: four nurses for more than 10 patients. You head back to the locker room and open your purse to reach for the aspirin for the headache that has already begun.

To most modern nurses, this scenario has an uncanny ring of familiarity. For practicing R.N. professionals, this situation depicts the commonplace in almost every American hospital in any city, in any state. Moreover, whether it be home health care, hospital, ambulatory care, or physician-office nursing, nurses are, collectively, in a crisis situation of major proportions.

For many years now, nurses have become all too familiar with the multitude of stresses incurred as a result of their choice of profession: long hours on their feet with no breaks, off-shift work, work on holidays and weekends, exposure to infectious disease, life-and-death decision making, moral and ethical dilemmas, the list goes on and on.

The preceding scenario is the embodiment of NURSE ABUSE, the overall deterioration of a once-noble profession. The elements which comprise and define NURSE ABUSE have been in existence as long as there have been nurses. However, it is only with the currently tumultuous state of nursing that NURSE ABUSE can be recognized as a serious and disabling phenomenon, a raging cancer-like growth, threatening to consume, destroy, and obliterate nursing as it now exists. In fact, NURSE ABUSE has ramifications so significant that it jeopardizes the health-care profession at large, as well as the welfare of the general public.

There are a variety of types of abuse that are well-documented, widely publicized, and familiar to the lay public: child abuse, woman abuse, sexual abuse, elder abuse, and substance abuse. However, until now, there have been only fragmented references to the "abuse" of nurses, although this phenomenon is becoming more frequently recognized both inside and outside the profession. Yet, little has been done to correct and eradicate the problem.

For the sake of simplicity, it would be easier to contrive a one-sentence definition of NURSE ABUSE, i.e., the mistreatment, neglect, exploitation, and devaluation of nurses. But to limit NURSE ABUSE in such a way would further compound its injustice. It is our fervent hope that this discussion will bring to the nursing and medical communities, as well as the larger public, a greater awareness of NURSE ABUSE in its entirety. Here, we will look at NURSE ABUSE as a disease, and the forms of abuse as its symptoms. Hopefully, it will inspire all those who care about this issue to reach deep within themselves for the cure.

Onset of Abuse: The Student Nurse

As is well known, women are predisposed to potential and actual abuse merely as a result of their 50:50 chance of being born female. Luckily, however, with the great strides accomplished by the feminist movement of the preceding decades, the mistreatment of the female population, although not eliminated, has in many instances been brought to the forefront of public awareness.

That notwithstanding, as women who are "weaker, subservient, and emotional," we are conditioned to be abused. As a result, the vulnerability to abuse is already in existence when young ingenues enter nursing school.

Call to mind, if possible, the thoughts that blossomed during your final years in high school when you made the choice of your "life's calling" to become a nurse. Your optimistic outlook and caring ideals propelled you toward the nursing role; your goal would be one of helping people, making them better, saving lives, and diminishing suffering.

You envisioned yourself sitting at a dying person's bedside, holding his or her hand, or comforting a crying child who awakened frightened in the middle of the night. You were well aware that needles, vomitus, and bedpans constituted the non-glamorous aspects of the job, but you were prepared to meet the physical, emotional, and intellectual challenges that nursing would provide.

Despite the fact that family members and "significant others" often questioned your career choice, ("You're too smart to be a nurse, why don't you be a doctor?"), you were prepared to face the challenges you thought nursing had to offer. But when you first walked through the hallowed halls of nursing academia, little did you know how unprepared you'd be for the true job of nursing.

No matter what type of basic preparation you may have had (i.e., a two-, three-, or four-year course of study,) nurses are united in their recollections of the nightmares endured in the quest to become a Registered Nurse or Licensed Practical Nurse. (Unfortunately that may be the only element that unifies these disparate groups).

From students working for the institutions in which they matriculated—providing coverage any time of the day or night and any day of the week— to the pupil subjected to the "all nighter," preparing the care plan for the next clinical day, the rigors and stressors were daunting, to say the least. It is well past time to take a serious look at what we are still doing to nursing students, in whom reside nursing's bright and promising future.

The student nurse is inaugurated into the realm of NURSE ABUSE the moment he or she accepts admission to an accredited school of nursing. Prior to the current crisis, when competition for entry into nursing school was fierce, only the best and brightest were fortunate enough to land a seat in the upcoming freshman class. Not only was it imperative to be academically qualified, it was also necessary to be a well-rounded and upstanding citizen, with demonstrated participation in extra-curricular activities.

It was, and is, from this moment on that the novice sacrifices his or her individualism on the altar of the greater good—the school— adopting, for the greater part of her academic life, the school's philosophy of nursing. Categorized by her fellow university colleagues as the "poor unfortunate nursing student," s/he is forced to give up her social life, corralled into classes starting at eight a.m., and then obliged to spend endless hours, after a full day of classes, in the library.

Usually rising at five o'clock in the morning to practice at the hospital, the nursing student is compelled to give up much-needed sleep in order to be prepared for clinical practice. You watch, with envy, your fellow collegians sleeping until a decent waking hour, and it makes you wonder whether the present sacrifices will be worth your eventual goal of being a nurse.

The intense academic requirements of nursing school are taken for granted by those who have endured it, but are totally unrecognized by those who have not. It is necessary to be educated in a multitude of academic disciplines: mathematics, biology, chemistry, microbiology, anatomy and physiology, pathophysiology, psychology, sociology, history, theology, and philosophy, not to mention the requirements designed to make a "well-rounded student." All this on top of the profusion of nursing educational courses required.

Academic requirements aside, the emotional and physical stress and ethical uncertainties to which the nurse-ingenue is subject are perhaps more subtle then the others, and therefore less dramatic in their impact. But these are important components to the reality of nursing, which are never sufficiently addressed in the academic curriculum of the nursing student. For every compassionate, empathic nursing instructor, there is one who is just as rigid, unyielding and unsympathetic. Exposing students to the reality of the nursing profession is one thing, but causing them a state of disequilibrium has caused many students to have nervous breakdowns, eating disorders, and suicidal ideation.

One university nursing instructor emphatically spoke these words: "We will, for the next four years, put you in a constant state of disequilibrium." She was dead serious. We know a nurse who had to call an all-night help line one night because a fellow nursing student told her she was considering committing suicide after flunking chemistry for the third time. This was before the nurse had gone through her psychiatric-nursing rotation, in which she learned the "correct" way of dealing with this kind of distress. Does it take this type of cold, hard reality to make us take a good hard look at what is being done to our nursing students?

Unrealistic "testing" criteria abound in nursing education. For example, take the student who receives a patient assignment on Thursday evening and is expected to prepare a full plan of care for her assigned patient by Friday morning at seven a.m. The result: a physically and emotionally exhausted nursing student.

One student was told she nearly failed her psychiatric-nursing rotation, not because of failing on a test or a poor academic performance, but "for failing to establish a therapeutic relationship" with a chronic-schizophrenic patient during her eight-week psychiatric rotation. Another student, who ruptured her appendix, was forced to return to school in one week and told: "There is no room for personal problems or misfortunes; if you miss too many clinical practices or classroom work, you will have to leave."

In discussing what nursing students endure, it is not our intention to criticize or censure nursing faculty gratuitously, but merely to bring to light common practices to which nursing students are routinely subjected that contribute to the proliferation of NURSE ABUSE. Although it purports to illustrate the reality of the work place, the teaching of nurses fails to expose the student-in-training to true work-related realities: shift rotation, weekend work, holidays, short staffing, excessive patient-to-nurse ratios, critical-care nursing, emotional stress, ethical dilemmas, and health-care-related business issues.

With many health-care agencies now being run by business professionals, not health-care professionals, it is imperative to teach nursing students principles of business practice. Also, more time must be allotted for clinical practice, even if it necessitates increasing existing programs by an additional year.

The status of the modern nursing student in the health-care environment is yet another subject that warrants immediate and drastic attention and intervention. It is at this formidable crossroad that nursing educators and staff personnel can jointly either make or break the nursing student. The fledgling nurse needs a friendly face, a sympathetic ear, a guiding hand in those impressionable early days of practice. Too often, s/he is treated as a third-class citizen by the hospital/institutional staff, and is compelled to carry out the more unpleasant duties of the experienced, but overworked and overstressed, staff nurse.

Frequently, the student is viewed as a hindrance rather than a help by the nursing staff because of the time required to explain procedures, policies, and other formalities of care. "I can do it in half the time myself," the experienced nurse might say. Unfortunately, the student is left feeling incompetent, and in the way. Even more serious is the fact that the student is often looked at as "an extra pair of hands," allowing administration to lull themselves into a false sense of staffing security, and convince one another that they managed to get by without another nurse, for just another day.

The profession of medicine, and members of some interdisciplinary departments, also prey upon the innocent nurse, who bears the brunt of their frustrations. It is sometimes made painfully evident to student nurses that the hospital staff does not want them there, and that patients' families do not want them there either. Another blow to the morale of the nursing student is the "You don't have it as bad as I did" mentality. The "I suffered through nursing school and so can you" sentiment is too often offered as some demented "rite of passage."

By giving a nursing student what they think is "reality" in the work place, some seasoned professionals are, in essence, destroying the new nurse's motivation, optimism, and idealism, and undermining him or her emotionally, shattering self-esteem and destroying a professional self concept before it has ever had an opportunity to thrive and grow.

Professional Abuse

Nurse-to-Nurse Abuse

The proverbial "line of demarcation" in the nurse-to-nurse relationship begins innocently enough as the result of the nursing profession's diverse preparatory educational background: the L.P.N.,

(Licensed Practical Nurse) vs. the R.N. (Registered Nurse, Diploma Graduate) vs. the R.N. (Associate Degree) vs. the R.N. (Baccalaureate Degree) vs. the R.N. (Master's Degree). The profusion of preparatory possibilities has promoted an ongoing rift among nurses that has been widening for years. The different programs that have been available for educating nurses were tailored to meet the individual's personal and socioeconomic needs, as well as the differing caregiver needs of institutions.

In the past, the argument was made that "a nurse is a nurse is a nurse." However, attempts to regulate entry-level educational requirements have made this thinking outdated. There has always been, to some degree, dissension among nurses because of their differing educational backgrounds. Today, L.P.N.s are finding their contribution increasingly valued by the institution, while R.N.s, once considered by the Joint Commission of Accredited Hospitals to be more cost-efficient, are increasingly laid-off by institutional policies of "cost containment."

Isn't it ironic how times change. In the 1980s, the R.N.'s value as a well-rounded, cost effective professional was the driving force behind the Total Patient Care delivery model. L.P.N.s and nursing assistants were devalued, laid off, and replaced with R.N.s. Today, in the '90s, there is a total reversal of that model, with economics being the one-and-only driving force in determining practice models.

R.N.s, however, are not just being laid-off, they are witnessing the total dismantling of their profession as greedy administrators have developed the strategy of de-licensing nursing activities. After all, if you don't need a license to perform complex nursing functions, then you don't need to pay an R.N. to take care of patients! In the end, patient morbidity and mortality will write yet another chapter in the story of NURSE ABUSE.

But more fundamental to this issue is the unrest among R.N.s.

The point of view held by many individual nurses, as well as "organized" nursing, is that the R.N. with a baccalaureate or master's degree is truly a nursing "professional." Diploma-degree nurses argue that they are the more technically skilled, because of their superior clinical experience. The B.S.N. nurses argue that, although their clinical practice may be lacking, their knowledge of theoretical principles makes them superior nurses. These disparate points of view set the stage for competitiveness and animosity among nurses, the nurse-to-nurse relationship inevitably suffers, and nurse-to-nurse abuse is perpetuated from within.

What is at the root of these contentious relationships? Is the problem intrinsic to a profession that is predominately female; is this just "girls being girls"? The answer, unfortunately, is not that simple. Ashley (1981, p. 3) writes that nurses continue to function in a patriarchal system, one in which nursing remains contained in a sexist profession. Patriarchy, she says, has its roots clearly entrenched in misogyny, or the hatred of women (Ashley, 1981, p. 3). And Reakes (1981, p. 8) says that "Sexism is an obstacle to realizing full development, and perpetuates the stereotypes of femininity and masculinity. Women incorporate male values and attitudes in the patriarchal system, and devalue other women's performances, attitudes, goals, and backgrounds."

Therein lies the dilemma. With its origin in patriarchy, nursing has continued to imitate and then perpetuate male behaviors and attitudes. Thus, nurse-to-nurse abuse continues to thrive. As a result, we are unable to realize our full potential, that of governing and controlling our profession, being at the helm of what transpires. Functioning in the sphere of a male-dominated profession—medicine—nurses continue to serve physicians and administrators and their feelings of frustration and powerlessness cause them to ventilate on that easily accessible target, the other nurse. Can this behavior be separate from the profession?

As we've already mentioned, the seeds of nurse-to-nurse abuse are planted in student nurses when they are introduced to the profession. Another example is what happens to the "new" staff nurse. Territorialism may be instinctive behavior, but with the addition of a new staff member to the nursing unit, the existing staff sometimes goes out of its way to make the new nurse feel miserable. The new nurse is usually evaluated by some hidden criteria of worthiness.

First impressions are of the utmost importance in helping people decide whether or not they will stay in a particular position. This type of initiation gauntlet is obviously not a way to establish positive first impressions. A different and more understanding approach would help considerably in decreasing one major component of the current crisis, staff turnover.

Scapegoating is another commonly-employed strategy in the nurse-to-nurse abuse syndrome. Let's face it, we are all, at one time or another, guilty of gossiping, placing blame elsewhere, or taking our frustrations out on other staff members. Because of the serious constraints imposed on nurses by the current nursing shortage, we frequently find ourselves falling short of our own personal and professional expectations, not only with respect to the kind of care we want to deliver to our patients, but to our image of ourselves as supportive of other nurses.

As a result, we place blame on each other and our colleagues bear the brunt of our frustrations. How many times have we rolled our eyes in disgust when we found we were taking report from Nurse So-and-So, the one who always leaves her rooms like disaster areas, her patients in pre-code condition, a list of "things-to-do" a mile long? Immediately addressing such interpersonal problems might help defuse the types of conflicts that often ignite when inadequate staffing, insufficient and outdated equipment, more critically ill patients, and lack of administrative support are commonplace.

The "generally competent" nurse who is able to function in a general med-surg setting, but unable to function adequately in a particular specialty area, is not commonly addressed in the nursing-administration arena. Compared to her peers in a specialty setting, this nurse does not or cannot practice in a prudent, knowledgeable, and professional manner, even after every educational and training opportunity has been offered. This issue has been and may continue to be a major source of persistent nurse-to-nurse abuse because of chronic shortages in specialty areas.

Administrators turn a deaf ear to nurses' concerns about a colleague who may not be equipped to handle responsibilities in a specialty area. For them, it's far easier to think in terms of a "warm body" who will fill a chronically vacant staffing slot. Inevitably, the anger nurses feel about this unfair situation is expressed, not to administration, but to their nurse colleagues. This is yet another example of nurse-to-nurse abuse.

Physician-to-Nurse Abuse

The nurse/physician relationship is frequently discussed, dissected, and lamented. Throughout the history of medicine, there has been a symbiotic relationship between nurses and physicians in which medicine has ultimately dominated. Although emancipated, to a certain degree, from the "handmaiden mentality," [nurses are under] the control, domination, intimidation, and nullification implicit in a system of medical patriarchy...many nurses do not recognize their abusive situation...." (Lovell, 1981, p 25).

Every day, in some way, shape, or form, nurses are abused by physicians. In one survey of nurse-physician relationships, Fried man concluded that nurses face a multitude of abuses from their non-nurse health-care colleagues: condescending attitudes; lack of respect, as either a person or professional; public humiliation as physicians rant and rave in front of patients, families, or anyone who will listen; temper tantrums of doctors who scream and throw things if unhappy about anything; scapegoating by blaming nurses for anything that goes wrong (or if the doctor is merely "in a bad mood"); failure to read nurses' notes or listen to nurses' suggestions; refusal to share information about patients; lack of understanding about what nurses do; frequent disparaging remarks in public (Cox, 1987, p. 47)

Imagine what would happen if a nurse were guilty of the same abusive behavior? It would never be tolerated! So why then do physicians continue this behavior without reproach? Nurses, themselves, must bear part of the responsibility for the perpetuation of NURSE ABUSE by physicians. Although nursing has evolved from a "servant" role to that of "interdisciplinary team member," nurses' significance in patient-care delivery remains at a level lower than that of "all-knowing, all-healing" physicians.

But nurses and doctors are co-professionals. The nurse's role is that of advocate, as s/he directs attention to all facets of THE PATIENT's care, and not to the physician.

Administration-to-Nurse Abuse

As significant as the abuse of nurses is by physicians and even other nurses, the phenomenon of NURSE ABUSE by administrators and the administration they serve is virtually unequalled. Once nurses have expressed their grievances about wages, hours, staffing, and respect, the cornerstone to NURSE ABUSE and those which bear the brunt of the responsibility are hospital, health-care institution, and nursing administration. Those who represent the bureaucratic, business-suit mentality, those who sit comfortably in their upholstered chairs behind their shiny mahogany desks, these are the people who are primarily responsible for the static state of the nursing profession today.

The administrative abuse of nurses emerges as the single most important, widespread, and commonly identified element found in surveys of nursing-job dissatisfaction. Nurses, who are equipped to and should be empowered to make decisions regarding optimal, holistic patient care, are being held fiscal hostages by their institutions. Their ability to implement change, to deliver the type of nursing care of which they are capable and which their patients deserve are all limited by budgetary constraints.

With the advent in recent years of Diagnostic-Related Groupings and reengineering, the assault on the nursing profession has become even more intense. Nursing positions have been cut, and lay-offs or defections have occurred at the very same time that hospital administrators are rewarded with company cars for their due diligence in "balancing the budget."

Nursing has become the "easy solution" for administrative hatchet men and women. When things get tough, nursing is inevitably singled out for staffing cutbacks. Amazingly, there seems to be a continued increase in the numbers and salaries of administrative positions, inspiring the oft-quoted platitude, found frequently among nurses: "There are too many Chiefs and not enough Indians."

What the business-mogul administrators did not count on, however, was what DRGs would lead to. Increased technology and technical skills, and ever-more sophisticated diagnostic-and-therapeutic treatment modalities have enabled the health-care system to save more patients. Many hospitals, rather than realizing a greater profit by increasing patient turnover, have found that DRGs, ironically, have lead to an increased need for skilled nurses who specialize in the care of patients confined to institutions for longer periods of time. Enter reengineering and "skill-mix" strategies, all designed to eliminate nursing positions.

These strategies, along with new hospital wings, improved diagnostic facilities, and advancement in health-care services have helped hospitals to attain financial profit and government grants.

And the institution's public image, achieved through aggressive community advertisement and promotion, is considered of utmost importance in achieving economic superiority. It is no wonder, then, that competition to attract the health-care consumer among facilities is so fierce.

Who is first in line to suffer at the hand of these bureaucratic tyrants? Patients! Who, then, is destined to follow? Nurses! Today, the health-care industry finds itself in a quandary. Currently, there are an insufficient number of nurses, and the demand is expected to rise over the next ten years, leading the public into a 21st Century in which the health-care industry will be inundated with even more elderly patients, and an unprecedented number of people afflicted with AIDS.

Administrators of both health-care, in general, and nursing, in particular, recognize the legitimate power within the nursing profession. But by patronizing nurses as if they were whining children, and by perpetuating their subservient, handmaiden stereotype, these administrators have been able to rob nurses of their legitimate power. To attain the position of significance they so justly deserve, nurses must unite, whether in structured, unionized groups, or as members of nursing organizations that are addressing important issues with seriousness and clout.

Administrative managers, and nursing administration itself, keep nurses bickering and fighting amongst themselves in order to keep them off-balance and ineffectual —the classic "divide and conquer" mentality. Their total lack of respect for the nursing profession is obvious in the ways in which they refuse to allow input from nurses about nursing-related issues.

In addition, rather than spending money to keep their institution's nurses content and optimally functional by improving wages, ancillary services, and benefit "perks," administrators spend millions to prevent nurses from unionizing. Clearly, they recognize the potential power in unionization, and fear a serious lack of control over nurses who are unionized.

The continued and abhorrent misuse of the nurse in the hospital setting is amply illustrated by the variety of roles the nurse is expected to assume everyday, roles that lie outside the realm of nursing. For instance:

1.   Housekeeper. Frequently, the nurse is responsible for moving and cleaning furniture (beds especially) in order to make room for more patients and thereby increase hospital revenue. Emptying overflowing waste baskets, dusting and cleaning patient-care areas, and cleaning monitors and equipment all fall, by default, to nurses.

2.   Secretary/clerical worker. Nurses must answer the phone, order supplies, and call different departments to track down those supplies, fill out lab slips, file lab reports, make out diagnostic procedure forms (and then obtain results), and contact other departments to get things accomplished. Voluminous paperwork, resulting from inadequate computerization, contributes greatly to the clerical role imposed upon nursing.

3.   Transporter/moving company. Nurses spend valuable time and energy moving patients to and from wheelchairs, stretchers, and beds, and transporting patients to other departments, to other floors, and out the door. The time spent looking for those vehicles is another misuse of nursing personnel.

4.   Dietician, physical therapist, respiratory therapist, and lab technician. The nurse ensures that the appropriate diet is ordered for the appropriate patient three times a day. Because of insufficient staffing in other patient-care areas, nurses are often compelled to perform the duties of the physical and respiratory therapist,

as well as the venipuncturist, dietician, social worker, etc.

5.   Police officer/security guard. In addition to insuring that their patients are in a "safe" environment, nurses are required to monitor the number of visitors, the frequency of visitors, and the length of time visitors stay with patients.

6.   Handyman. Nurses, by necessity, have become quite versatile in their ability to troubleshoot and fix malfunctioning equipment. They've become equally adept at teaching the engineering and maintenance departments how to troubleshoot and fix malfunctioning equipment.

7.   Nursing supervisor. Everyday, nurses evaluate patient-care needs, deciding how many staff nurses are needed to care for how many patients. The irony here is that they must then substantiate and explain their decisions to the REAL nursing supervisor. So far removed from patient care are "nurse administrators," they should be forever indebted to nurses on the "frontlines" who help them per form their jobs adequately. It is the bedside nurse who is, in reality, the true nursing supervisor.

NURSE ABUSE is further fostered by nursing executives and managers (collectively nursing administrators), who dictate nursing practice. By utilizing computer software that cranks out "patient acuity" data, a numerical value given to designate the amount of care patients require, nursing executives and managers are able to sit behind their desks and decide how many nurses there should be to take care of "X" number of patients. However, these data measure routine tasks, not emergencies, family interactions, preparation of patients for diagnostic procedures, etc., all of which occur frequently.

It is obvious that decisions about patient care should be made by staff nurses at the beside, not nursing administrators who, by merely reading a patient's name and diagnosis from a report sheet, believe they are equipped to dictate the level needed of nursing care. This is demeaning to nurses and contributes to the flagrant demoralization that supervisors inflict with impunity.

Another problem is the administrators' faulty perception of the realities of nursing practice, their belief that nurses are interchangeable, that an emergency room nurse, for instance, can just as easily work on a pediatric unit "in a pinch." Although it is the administrator's job to ensure the delivery of safe patient care, and although safe patient care is usually delivered, it is frequently at the nurse's expense.

Specifically, the "Float the Nurse" game is played when a nurse who normally works on one unit is sent to another area to provide adequate nursing coverage. If s/he is "lucky," s/he will be sent to an area similar to that in which s/he practices. Many times, however, this is not the case. This situation can and does have serious legal ramifications. Although nurses have a basic educational foundation, nursing has become so diversified and specialized that a nurse can jeopardize both career and license by working in an area in which s/he lacks appropriate training.

The nurse who gets "floated" is usually one with a higher level of nursing skill and expertise, and so the one more frequently abused by the institution to fill in the empty "slots." Increased levels of experience and knowledge do not necessarily make it safer for the patient if the nurse caring for that patient is practicing outside his or her area of expertise. This matters little to nursing supervisory personnel.

Yet another dangerous and negligent practice among the administrative hierarchy is the popular game called the "Revolving Door." In many institutions, little concern is given to the numbers of patients, the type of nursing care required, and the number of nurses needed to deliver such care. Instead, the object of the game is FILL

THE BEDS. It is, after all, bad business practice to turn patients away, even if the beds are full to capacity. By filling the hallways, doubling patients up in single rooms, or sending patients out of intensive-care units in the middle of the night, the hospital can increase patient census, and consequently increase revenue. Again, the nurse is the last to be considered.

Hospital and nursing administrators insist that "it doesn't look good to the public" to close emergency rooms to patient admissions, or to transfer patients to another health-care facility. No concern whatsoever is given to the number of nurses available to ensure safe patient care. The charge nurse will state emphatically to the nursing supervisor: "We don't have enough nurses!" The supervisor, in turn, will usually respond with a perfunctory: "You'll have to `make do' with what you have; you should be able to handle that many patients."

In this situation, psychological warfare explodes. Nurses are made to feel that, if they are "good nurses," they should be able to care for their patients, no matter how many there are. On the other hand, some hospital and nursing administrators are telling practicing professionals that their levels of nursing practice are too high. There is no greater slap in the face than to be told by the Director of Nursing that, "You girls need to reevaluate your standards of practice, they are too high. Nursing is changing!"

What is the price, then, of human life? If it were the loved one of the hospital or nursing administrator lying in that hospital bed, there would not be any standard of care "too high" for them. Are nurses, then, destined to lower their level of practice, spreading themselves ever-thinner among ever-larger numbers of patients, in order to ensure that the institution's tallies at the end of the fiscal year are "in the black"? It is about time that levels of nursing care be determined by NURSES! No longer should these financial henchmen and women be permitted to perpetuate these heinous and abusive acts against nurses and patients.

Physical and Environmental Abuse of Nurses

Nurses physically abused? Preposterous! Or is it? Certainly, there may not be broken bones, unsightly scars, blackened eyes, or any of the other physical signs often seen in someone who is the victim of physical abuse or violence. The physical abuse of nurses is so much more subtle and insidious. Unfortunately, not enough attention is focused on this form of NURSE ABUSE.

Far too many nurses have known the reality of the most frequently-identified hazard in the job of professional nursing, back injury. Long hours on their feet and extended overtime shifts contribute significantly to the wear and tear on the bodies of nurses. Coupled with insufficient numbers of staff available for assistance, and the lack of equipment to mobilize patients, it is inevitable that back injuries occur. One study estimated that in the span of one hour's work, two nurses lifted the equivalent of two-and-a-half tons of patient weight on the nursing unit on which they worked!

In another study "of more than 500 staff nurses, 52 percent said they had work-related back pain that lasted longer than 14 days. These nurses were young (83 percent were under the age of 30). Those who had suffered from back pain traced it to three activities: lifting a patient in bed, helping a patient get out of bed, and moving a bed" (Gates, 1988, p. 656). Moreover, wherever there is a shortage of nurses, injuries flourish, all despite the conscientious use of proper body mechanics.

Although back injury is the most common injury to nurses, other orthopedic problems are well documented. Injuries such as cervical strain, tendinitis, foot and leg ailments, varicosities and corns occur frequently. And what becomes of these ill-fated nurses who have the audacity to become injured? They are labeled by the institution or agency for which they work as a liability. From the institutional perspective of risk management, the injured nurse is just that, a risk. Rather than investigate the causative event and variables, the institution interprets the injury as being the fault of the nurse, and expects that the responsibility for any physical damage should be sustained by that nurse.

Furthermore, when it comes to the issue of monetary compensation for illness or injury incurred on the job, nurses get a raw deal because they are seen as being dispensable. It would behoove health-care institutions to spend money on necessities like patient lifting equipment and ancillary staff, or to safely staff nursing units with MORE nurses. From a risk-management perspective, these remedies, in and of themselves, would help to decrease the number of work-related injuries and Workmen's Compensation expenditures.

Another seldom-discussed, but prevalent, form of physical abuse sustained by nurses results from combative patients. Ask any Emergency Department nurse on a Saturday night shift if s/he was physically abused and you will hear a resounding YES! Ask any psychiatric nurse, ask any medical-surgical nurse, the list goes on and on. Physical injury to nurses occurs at the hands of the confused, the bereaved, the psychotic, or the drug- or alcohol-intoxicated patient.

Physical abuse consists of harm in the form of punches, kicks, strangulation attempts, bites, and scratches. The literature discusses ways in which to handle physically abusive and potentially life-threatening patients, but there is no discussion of the hospital's role in preventing these abuses or helping nurses who have been assaulted to deal with the aftermath.

Some time ago, we were engaged in a conversation about NURSE ABUSE and the man to whom we were speaking asked: "Well, isn't that part of your job? Isn't that just a work-related hazard? Isn't that what your pay compensates you for?" Unfortunately, he was not (and is not) alone in his ignorance. His is a point of view shared by far too many. Nurses need to make people aware.

Shift work, a mandatory component of the nursing profession, is also a contributory factor to physical abuse. Much has been written about circadian rhythms and the effect that shift rotation plays on the body's intrinsic biological time clock. Some studies have shown that after several years of rotating shifts, workers' general health problems appear earlier than who work days. Other studies have shown that gastrointestinal disease occurs earlier in three-shift workers, and that the incidence of myocardial infarction relates directly to the amount of exposure to shift work (Janowski, 1988, p. 1337).

People require nursing care 24-hours a day, seven days a week, 52-weeks a year, so, for nurses it is impossible for shift work to become obsolete. However, shift work would be less physically detrimental if employers followed guidelines and recommendations by experts in the fields of sleep and circadian rhythms. Based on a review of research into various shift-rotation systems, sleep-expert Torbjorn Akerstedt of Sweden suggests several shift strategies: a short-night shift (six to eight hours), clockwise rotation (days to evenings to nights) with nights at the end of the series, and a slow rotation (four to seven days) (Janowski, 1988, p. 1341).

Today, mandatory overtime is becoming a more frequent means of staffing understaffed units, with many nurses mandated to work double shifts. Not only is mandatory overtime sanctioned in contractual language, the built-in guilt most nurses feel makes them unable to turn their backs when patients' lives may be in jeopardy. It is not only physically exhausting to work 16 consecutive hours in a high-pressured job, it may also prove dangerous. When nurses need their judgment to be flawless, their physical conditions play a major role.

A nurse, or any person for that matter, is more apt to make an error, or to overlook a crucial observation, if s/he is physically exhausted. In a profession where an error can cause serious or fatal consequences, working under these conditions jeopardizes not only the nurse's license, but, more importantly, the patient's welfare. And what of "break" times, mandated by law for working eight hours? These necessary rest periods are becoming fewer and farther between, as nurses find it nearly impossible to take much-needed break time because there simply are no people available to relieve them. Rather than pay staff members who are compelled to work through their allotted break time, more and more facilities have chosen to eliminate the "break" by shortening off-shifts to eight hours only.

The nursing staff is, therefore, entitled to only a five-to-ten minute break every four hours, as determined by their state laws. In addition, the eight-hour shift inevitably becomes a nine or 10 or 11 hour shift, and 12-hour shifts extend to thirteen, as nurses stay late, often without remuneration, constantly striving to accomplish everything required by their patients.

Budgetary compliance being a must, institutions require nurses to all but prostitute themselves to receive compensation for total hours worked. This is illustrated in the example of the institution that requires its nurses to notify their supervisor if they will not be finished on time, to fill out a form stating the reason for the "tardiness," and to have it approved by the nursing supervisor.

If this protocol is not followed, the nurses do not receive payment for the overtime worked. For the nurse who doesn't finish his or her work on time, a slap on the wrist is in order and s/he is told by supervisory personnel that s/he is incapable of utilizing her time efficiently.

One final bone of contention is the ever-elusive goal of permanent, steady, day-shift hours once the status of seniority has been achieved. Nurses continue to be scheduled to work both the day and night shifts in a five-day work week. Hence, the perpetuation of the physical abuse of nurses continues.

The above examples represent the overt, physical dangers to nurses in the hospital environment. But what of the less obvious ones, those that lurk in every nook and cranny of the hospital and health-care facility? According to one estimate, 60 percent of all health-care workers are regularly exposed to numerous toxic chemicals, ranging from the obvious dangers, such as the formaldehyde used in the lab and morgue, to common cleaning solutions used all over the hospital everyday (Leonard, 1988, p. 59).

And what of the other hazards: X-ray machines, radiation implants, radioisotopes used for tests, or the anesthetic gases nurses come in contact with? All pose serious health risks, including genetic malformations, sterility, and cancer. In addition, exposure to certain drugs can cause those who handle them adverse affects, cytotoxic and chemotherapeutic agents being the most devastating offenders. Something as seemingly benign as bone cement, used in the operating room during orthopedic procedures, can cause respiratory tract ailments and be potentially carcinogenic. Even the anesthetic agents exhaled by patients in the recovery room can cause massive damage to a nurse's liver upon repeated exposure.

Bacterial and viral agents are abundant in the health-care environment. Exposure through blood, sputum, and excrement results in nurses being vulnerable to infectious or contagious diseases. The increased occurrence of hepatitis B is well documented. However, many institutions continue to refuse to vaccinate their employees against this debilitating disease. The AIDS epidemic has had a profound impact on nursing. Health-care workers take a risk, not so much with the diagnosed patient but with the undiagnosed. A major shift in behavior and thinking is necessary in order to consider everyone as being potentially infectious.

Fortunately, the Occupational Safety and Health Administration (OSHA) has expanded regulations to cover hospital workers on the job. "Right-to-know" regulations compel hospitals to enact programs for employees to be informed of the work environment hazards to which they are exposed. Among them are:

*   The right to have a material safety- data sheet describing the contents of a product and the hazards involved provided on request.

*   The right to receive thorough education about potentially hazardous chemicals workers come in contact with.

*   The right to have appropriate protective equipment—goggles, face masks, or respirators, for example, available for use when handling chemicals.

Health-care workers must know their rights and make their institutions responsible for providing this information to them. Physically and environmentally speaking, the poor design and structure of nursing units and patient-care areas is another example of NURSE ABUSE. Billions of dollars are spent for the architectural designs and construction of "state-of-the-art" health-care facilities, but without the input of the people who work in those areas most frequently, NURSES!

Cramming the greatest number of people into the smallest possible space for the least amount of money seems to be the goal of most institutions. Serious attempts must be made to take into account the environmental, as well as physical, needs of the nurses who staff these units. With nurses working 24-hours-a-day, their opinions and recommendations about design and construction should be given the highest possible consideration.

Emotional and Ethical Stresses and Abuse

Few other professionals experience the breadth of human

emotions felt by registered professional nurses, and few are confronted by the ethical decision-making dilemmas thrust upon nurses each day, many of life-and-death importance. These difficult and sophisticated decisions must be based on sound scientific, psychological, emotional, and ethical principles.

The emotional stress and ethical agonizing nurses face, day in and day out, contribute substantially to NURSE ABUSE. To be sure, there is an extremely fine line between what some describe and interpret as stress, and what others believe is abuse. Most nurses make a clear distinction between the two.

Nurses have the same emotions as other human beings, and so they inevitably become attached to their patients and/or their patients' families. As a result, if a patient suffers from an irreversible disease, the nurse, too, often suffers. The nurse hurts, cries, mourns, despite the stereotype that paints him or her as an emotionless or cold person.

As an example, patients depend on nurses for their emotional needs, as well as for their physical well being. It is not uncommon, however, for patients to associate nurses with their discomfort and pain, bad hospital food, lack of supplies, lack of progress, etc. Families often plead with the nurse: "Save my loved one, help me decide what to do, help me with the doctor." In addition to dealing with disease, suffering, and death on a daily basis, nurses encompass so many different facets—helping to bring a child into the world, saving a life, easing the pain of the dying. It is little wonder they are emotionally drained and stressed. It comes with the territory.

We know when we become nurses we will shoulder a variety of emotional experiences. By citing the emotional stress placed on nurses by patients and their families, we are not placing blame; rather, we are simply pointing out some of the contributing factors to the emotional stress nurses experience.

In the present state of nursing, yet another type of emotional stress is widespread. The nursing shortage has forced nurses to cut corners in order to save time, taking care of larger numbers of sicker patients. As a result, nurses experience feelings of inadequacy from trying to fulfill all the needs of their patients, but being unable to accomplish this. Nurses feel rage at those who attempt to undermine their goals and their idealism. They end up backstabbing and scapegoating their colleagues, which leads to even more stress. This stress is further fueled by nursing supervisors and administrators who compound the problem by making light of nurses' legitimate grievances and the emotions they feel.

As discussed before, two major culprits of the emotional abuse of nurses are nursing administrators and physicians. Nursing administration, for example, will invariably try to make the nurse who calls in sick feel guilty: "There will only be two nurses for fifty patients!" the supervisor will say. "You're leaving us short staffed; I won't be able to find anyone to replace you." If a nurse attempts to take time off for a vacation, or if s/he refuses to do an overtime shift, s/he will be accused by the supervisor of "depriving" her fellow nurses and her patients because of her "selfishness."

Physicians contribute to nurses' emotional stress and abuse in a number of ways and, more often than not, it is abuse that typifies the physician-nurse relationship. Physicians scream at nurses, insult them ("Find me someone around here who knows what they're doing!"), belittle them in front of colleagues and others ("I'm the doctor!"); and patronize them. Often, they ignore the advice of nurses, offending both their intelligence and expertise.

Doctors accuse nurses of being "too emotional," interpreting the nurse's genuine empathy as "unprofessional" (while exhibiting little if any emotion themselves). These types of behaviors feed into the already diminished sense of worth nurses have, and tend to make them think they are, indeed, less worthy and that their opinions, philosophies, feelings, and perceptions are less valid than those of the "more important" health-care worker, the doctor.

For nurses, the stress from emotional abuse is certainly not eclipsed by the stress that goes along with making ethical decisions. With advanced technology and diagnostic sophistication, the population grows older and lives longer. As a result, nurses are faced with more frequent ethically-charged and emotionally-wrought dilemmas, providing the perfect medium for what can be considered "ethical stress."

In everyday practice, the nurse is engaged in a virtual tug-of-war, trying, on the one hand, to make the "right" decision for his or her patients, and balancing, on the other hand, legal, moral, and ethical considerations. Consider the patient who begs the nurse to allow him to die. Frequently, the family or physician (or both) refuse to "give up" on the patient and allow nature to take its course. The nurse is bound to uphold the wishes of the family and the physician, or be faced with possible legal consequences. The patient's wishes are often ignored, and the nurse is compelled to "save" the patient by instituting resuscitative or invasive procedures—this, despite, the fact that the patient may have communicated otherwise.

Nurses spend 24-hours-a-day caring for patients and witnessing their suffering on a far more consistent basis than do either doctors and families, who spend a relatively small portion of time at the bedside. This is just one more example of the emotional stress nurses sustain.

The responsibility nurses feel for policing other members of the health-care team, particularly physicians, is another example of an ethics-associated stressor. The nurse must ensure that all physicians' orders are appropriate, that procedures are carried out with the utmost of care and technical skill, and that any incompetencies are reported. In one intensive-care unit, a staff nurse brought to the attention of a physician (still in training) that he had performed a minor invasive procedure with less than optimal sterile procedure.

The nurse believed this to be a matter of some significance to this patient, who was already very ill and highly susceptible to infection. The doctor's response to the nurse was: "Well, if you GIRLS hadn't asked the resident to perform the procedure, there wouldn't have been any problem! It's your fault!"

So even when the nurse does the right thing, she is found to be wrong! The fine line that exists between ethical stress and abuse is crossed when, after questioning a physician's order that the nurse knows from knowledge and experience to be incorrect, s/he is told by the physician to carry it out anyway. In this situation, the nurse has two options: carry out the order s/he knows to be wrong, or refuse to do so and face the consequences of his or her "insubordination."

Here is another example of the ethical abuse of nurses. You are the charge nurse on a nursing unit which is dangerously under-staffed and are told by the Emergency Department to expect two very sick patients. You know you can't possibly accept these pa-tients without receiving more nursing personnel, so you notify your nursing supervisor who tells you no additional nurses are available. She says you have no choice and must admit the patients to your floor.

The dynamics of this situation lead to ethical abuse for sev-eral reasons. The nurse is being forced to do what s/he knows is wrong and compelled to put her nursing license, personal integrity, and principles on the line, not to mention the lives of the patients s/he and her colleagues are caring for. The right thing to do would be to admit these patients because they need and deserve medical care. The wrong thing would be to give less-than-sufficient nursing care and jeopardize their lives. It would also be ethically wrong for the nurse to threaten to leave, thereby "abandoning" the patients.

Two rather simple strategies might address these issues ef-fectively: the inclusion of ethics courses in nursing curricula, and the presence of ethics committees in health-care settings where nurses practice.

The Financial Abuse of Nurses

The following provides a brief overview of the types of financial abuses nurses endure. The solutions to these abuses are evident. Only active, informed, and involved nurses can effect change in the injustices of this kind of NURSE ABUSE.

1.   <u>Wages and Raises.</u>

Despite salary gains, especially in the past few years, there is still a lack of adequate compensation for the number of years of education, experience, and skill professional nurses have in the healthcare system. Comparatively, nursing has failed to keep step with other professions in salary growth. Additionally, nurses are often at the mercy of their employers when it comes to raises. If no bargaining-unit contract is in existence, nursing salaries are governed by merit raises or cost-of-living increases, at best; at one hospital without a contract, nurses had no raise in an 18-month period. Many readers may know of even more outrageous financial abuses.

2.   <u>Benefits and "Perks".</u>

In this area, the old adage, "You don't get something for nothing" holds true. In order to enjoy increased hourly or weekly wages, nurses often find their benefit packages progressively being chipped away. Decreases in such benefits as tuition reimbursement and holiday pay often follow. Finally, decreases in the employer's payment of health insurance premiums may be the final sacrifice nurses must make in order to obtain increased wages.

3.   <u>Educational Reimbursements.</u>

It has been well-documented that the federal government's educational-loan program has suffered a substantial decline over the past several years. It is only with the current nursing shortage that some nursing-education support programs and loans have been re-enacted by legislators. Institutional tuition reimbursement has frequently fallen by the wayside. Advanced nursing degrees and certification in nursing specialty areas are also not compensated for monetarily in many areas of health care, despite professional and administrative pressure to achieve higher levels of educational and professional expertise.

In addition, in order to obtain nursing licensure renewal, it is mandated that nurses show proof of continuing education units (CEUs) and seminar attendance. Often, payment for these programs comes right out of the nurse's own pocket. If any reimbursement to nurses is given at all, it is dependent upon the good graces of the institution or health-care agency.

4.   Child Care.

Unfortunately, the employers of nurses still fall considerably behind other businesses in providing on-site child-care services for their employees. Shift work, notoriously associated with the nursing profession, makes it extremely difficult for nurses to find suitable child-care services within the community. The continued inflexibility of work schedules and lack of creative staffing patterns in health-care agencies also contribute significantly to the financial abuse of nurses with regard to obtaining child-care services.

5.   Agency or Temporary Nurses.

Health-care facilities continue to pay exorbitant fees for agency nurses, those versatile individuals who are able to "plug-in" to any institution at any particular time to meet staffing demands. It remains a bone of contention for the hospital staff nurse to work side by side with an agency nurse who, many times, is earning double the hourly wage. If institutions would pay their own nursing staff more money and increase ancillary services, they would improve job satisfaction and thereby increase employee loyalty.

6.   The Clinical Ladder or Career Ladder.
This is one of the more recent attempts to "keep nurses happy." Additional dollars, in the form of a percentage of hourly wage, is given to nurses for the work they do. With monetary compensation used as bait, nurses must provide written documentation of the work they do in order to receive this compensation. Rather than be given automatic compensation for the multifaceted services they provide, nurses must submit "proof" of their worthiness in order to receive more money.

Instead of automatically being addressed in terms of hourly wage or weekly compensation, this becomes a matter of who can submit the most impressively completed forms. Worse, it often degenerates into a personality contest. Many nurses view the "clinical ladder" as an insult to their intelligence.

Media and Public Abuse of Nurses

The Show: All My Children, ABC-TV
The Setting: The waiting room, Pine Valley Hospital
The Players: Dr. Joe Martin, Tad Martin, Nurse Eileen
The Subject: NURSE ABUSE

Dr Martin, standing near the nurse's station, is engaged in conversation with his son, Tad. Nurse Eileen, nurse's cap affixed to her head and wearing her off-white television-vanilla uniform, approaches the pair. The following conversation ensues.

Nurse Eileen: Dr. Martin?

Dr. Martin: Yes?

Nurse Eileen: Excuse me but I need to talk to you.

Dr. Martin:	Certainly, ah, oh, Eileen, this is my son Tad. (Turns to Tad). Eileen is one of our best nurses.
Tad:	I can see that! (Looks the nurse up and down).
Nurse Eileen:	Pleased to meet you.
Tad:	You, too! (Leers at her).
Dr. Martin:	(Turns to nurse) What's the problem?
Nurse Eileen:	It's Mr. Peterson in 309. He's complaining of chest pains. We've done E.K.G.'s (Electrocardiogram). We've monitored him but nothing shows up. I'm at a loss as to what's wrong.
Dr. Martin:	Hmmm. Mrs. Quinn is on duty, isn't she?
Nurse Eileen:	Yes, sir.
Dr. Martin:	Why don't you consult with her. She's very good at that sort of thing. I'm not familiar with the case and it would be improper for me to advise.
Nurse Eileen:	I'm sorry Dr. Martin, it's just, well, I always feel you have the answer that counts. Sorry for the interruption.
Nurse leaves.	Tad Martin turns to his father.

Tad:	Must be tough.
Dr. Martin:	What?
Tad:	Oh, being the idol of all these gorgeous young nurses!
Dr. Martin:	She just asked a question, Tad. Strictly routine.
Tad:	I could get used to a routine like that!

While hospital and nursing administrators insidiously erode the status of the nursing profession from within, the media's public abuse of the nurse contributes significantly to erosion from without. It is difficult to determine which element poses the greater threat to nursing's image, and hence the perpetuation of NURSE ABUSE nurses themselves, doctors, or the media. Clearly, all play an important role.

As the conversation from the television show "All My Children" illustrates, media abuse of nursing continues even in this day and age. But first, let's look briefly at the historic evolution of nursing from a public perspective, and discuss the role of the media as it affects nursing today.

The early role of nursing can be traced to the beginning of recorded history, and has always been closely linked to the art of mothering. "Innate materialism and womanly qualities were viewed as essential characteristics of the ideal nurse" (Hughes, 1980, p. 55). Those qualities intrinsic to the ideal mother—nurturing, caregiving, gentleness and daintiness, influenced by Victorian ideologies about women—constituted in the eyes of the public all of the attributes that nurses should possess. Aggression, competitiveness, and resistance to male authority were viewed as unbecoming and especially foreign to both the female and nursing role.

Although the first "nurses" were considered "immoral" women, such as prostitutes and drunks, the inception of formalized nurses' training in the late 1800's did little to elevate the job of nursing to a higher level of public admiration. Early nursing work was in a class no better than and, in fact, lower than that of a servant. With the establishment of training schools in the United States, the public image of the nurse underwent a slow process of change" (Hughes, 1980, p. 60).

Associated as a womanly profession of the Victorian era, the ideal nurse was depicted in literature as a true example of womanhood. It is from this point on that the social perspective of nursing took on a new look, that of the impeccably neat, well-groomed, polite, and pleasant young woman in a starched white uniform and cap.

Pleasing in personality and intellectually inferior to the all-knowing (predominantly male) physician, the concept of the nurse-as-handmaiden was born. This was the image portrayed to the public in the early 1900s, and the image the public still, to some degree, holds to be true. There was little notice given to the intellectual, cognitive and educational capabilities of the nurse administering to the patient. Rather, "that she be polite, well-spoken and as strong as an ox" was considered more important.

Over the years, nursing has evolved significantly: nurses have become significantly more educated, more accountable (i.e., carriers of independent malpractice insurance), more skilled, more diverse, and more independent. Yet, in spite of these genuine gains, they are still, according to the "public image," the mindless, sweet, sometimes overbearing "Angels of Mercy."

The public's beliefs about the nurse's role, which is reinforced by media depictions (such as "All My Children") have prevented the growth and understanding of what nursing really is, and what nurses really do. The public still believes that nurses wear caps and white uniforms, largely because the media still portray nurses (especially on television) with all the old stereotypes intact. Not understanding that nurses may be more concerned about their irregular heart beat, bleeding ulcer, medication dosage, or fluid-and-electrolyte balance, the public still demands a back rub and a box of tissues!

Unfortunately, nursing practice, in the eyes of the public, has been forever linked to medical practice. It is the public's belief that nurses are merely the extension of physicians, that nurses act dutifully only upon orders mandated by doctors. "To the detriment of the public and nursing profession alike, the public has never identified nursing care as separate and distinct from physician care" (Hughes, 1980, p. 68).

"The mythical belief in the nurse's subordination to the physician, projected through the popular media, has led to public depreciation of the role of the nurse in health care. Nursing care has always existed with or without physician supervision. The failure of the public to recognize this has had a damaging effect upon the growth of nurses as professional practitioners and upon the utilization of nurses to their fullest potential in health care" (Hughes, 1980, p. 69).

As responsible as the public-at-large is for its continued misunderstanding of the nursing image, the media is primarily responsible for "fueling the fire." At the onset of the 20th Century, the media portrayed nurses as "Angels of Mercy." In the 1920s, the "Nurse as Girl Friday" was in vogue. During World War II, the heroine nurse evolved, and post-war to 1965 the nursing image was synonymous with "wife and mother."

Yet, in the past two-and-a-half decades, the most negative and damaging image of nursing has emerged the nurse as sex object. Responsible for portraying nurses as sex-starved nymphomaniacs are the television and movie world, as well as greeting card companies. Since the late 1960s, the dumb, blond, bombshell nurse in a short, tight, low-cut uniform became the standard in spoofs of the profession. The nurse has commonly been seen chasing a male patient around his hospital room, or chasing the physician around the hospital. If not chasing men, she is seen hopping into bed (with either the patient or the doctor!)

Nurses are depicted as sensual, frivolous, irresponsible, and promiscuous. The primary plot in TV shows depicts the nurse both emotionally and sexually involved with her male patients (doctors, interns, residents), or fighting a substance-abuse problem.

One particularly offensive example was the TV series "Nightingales" (NBC-TV) which depicted a group of men and women as they began their journey through nursing school. So offensive were the stereotypes of nurses that, for one of the first times in nursing history, all nurses throughout the country, including organizations and individuals, succeeded through lobbying in having the show taken off the air. If nurses joined together to combat other forms of abuse, it would not exist.

Even with the addition of the new series, "ER," the stereotypes remain. The nurses in this television drama are portrayed as more intelligent, more competent, and more as central members of the health-care team. However, their roles still took a back seat to the ever-glorified physician until members of the Emergency Nurses Association succeeded in educating the producers about what nurses really do. Working closely with the writers and actors on the show, the ED nurses have made a significant difference and given the public perhaps its first "real" view of the nursing profession, in all of its talent and glory. Again, we have an example of nurses working together to combat abuse. When will this mentality "catch on" and become the rule and not the exception?

By contrast, the show "Chicago Hope" is possibly the worst "modern" television series ever filmed. One episode in particular focused entirely on a nurse's right to question and refuse to carry out an order which would have been detrimental to the patient's welfare. This situation occurs thousands of times a day in the real world, where nurses are required to be patient advocates by their State Nurse Practice Acts! But at the conclusion of this episode, the nurse was told she was never to even think about challenging a physician's order, despite the fact she was correct in her assessment.

Yet another episode of Chicago Hope revolved around a nurse who was deliberately set up by a physician for a sexual harassment lawsuit. Nurses are rarely, if ever, shown taking care of patients and exercising their many skills. If shown at all, they stand behind a nurses' station and act subservient to any physician who happens to be in the area.

Today's media stereotypes promote a negative perception of over two-million health-care providers—nurses. Nurse characters are presented as generally less important and less committed to their profession than physicians, and all-too-eager to enter into frivolous sexual liaisons. The nurse is almost always cast in a subordinate and demeaning role, portrayed as if she made far fewer contributions to the patient's well-being and was not capable of autonomous judgment.

In its depiction of nurses, the media make it almost impossible to separate fact from fiction, therefore creating a spurious, but dangerous, "reality" in the minds of the public. Since the media do not portray nurses as health-care providers instrumental to the patient's well being, and since they have failed to mirror the changing role of the nurse, the public lacks awareness of the many vital services that nurses provide.

Given the fact that the profession of nursing serves the public, nurses should be concerned about what the public thinks of them. Changes in media portrayals of nurses and nursing are both neces sary and possible. Nurses must voice their opinions and work actively to change negative media images into vital, positive, and accurate ideas of today's nursing profession.

Nurses need to become more politically involved by writing letters to (or for!) newspapers and magazines, lobbying legislators, protesting to (and boycotting) advertisers, and refusing to watch the television show/attend the movie/buy the products sold by the corporate sponsors of these outlandish media depictions that continue to demean the nursing image.

In addition, nurses must voice their outrage at the gross injustices that continue as a result of persistent media exploitation. It is only then that nurses will stop the flagrant distortions that, to this date, persist in the public consciousness.

This chapter represents our efforts in defining some of the special issues, problems, and barriers confronting nurses today. Many of the abuses we have written about are ones we have experienced personally, as have many of our colleagues. The emotional and political issues we've discussed can, we believe, be resolved in a constructive and rational manner. First, however, an awareness of these problems must be developed. We hope this chapter has delineated many of nursing's problems, and inspired our readers to be a part of their solution.

References

Ashley, J. (1981). Power in Structured Misogyny: Implications for the Politics of Care. *Advances in Nursing Science*, 3(3), 3-22.

Bennett, J. (1985). AIDS Epidemiology Update. *American Journal of Nursing*, September, 968-971.

Cox, H. (1987). Verbal Abuse In Nursing: Report of a Study. *Nursing Management*, November, 47-50.

Friedman, F.B. (1982). A Nurse's Guide to the Care and Handling of M.D.'s. *RN*, March, 39-43.

Gates, S. (1988). On-the-Job Back Exercises. *American Journal of Nursing*, May, 656-659.

Hughes, L. (1980). The Public Image of the Nurse. *Advances in Nursing Science*, 2(2), 55-71.

Janowski, M.J. (1988). More from the Night Owls. *American Journal of Nursing*, October, 1337-1341.

Leonard, D. (1988). What Hospitals Must Tell You About Work Hazards. *RN*, February, 59-62.

Lovell, M. (1981). Silent but Perfect Partners: Medicine's Use and Abuse of Women. *Advances in Nursing Science*, 3(2), 25-39.

Reakes, J. (1981). Nurse Abuse. *Texas Nursing*, October, pgs. 8-9.

Chapter Four

ANOTHER LOOK AT BURNOUT

by Kathy McMahon, R.N., M.S.N.

Few will deny that nursing is a stressful occupation. By any measure, the demands made on nurses are excessive. It seems logical, then, that when these stresses continue undiminished and without relief, "Burnout" is bound to occur.

Professional burnout, as defined in the *Cumulative Index of Nursing and Allied Health Literature*, is "An excessive stress reaction to one's occupational or professional environment. It is manifested by feelings of emotional and physical exhaustion, coupled with a sense of frustration and failure."

Cherniss (1987, p. 55) described burnout simply as "negative changes in work-related attitudes and behavior in response to job stress." He elaborated by defining burnout to include "increasing discouragement, pessimism, and fatalism about one's work; decline in motivation, effort, and involvement in work; apathy; negativism; frequent irritability and anger with clients and colleagues;...resistance to change, growing rigidity, and loss of creativity" (Firth, 1986, p. 634).

My own definition of burnout, based on personal experience as a nurse, would be "a depressed or apathetic state on the part of the caretaker due to unreasonably high expectations in an unreasonably short period of time". What happens to the enthusiasm, excitement, and caring that the new nurse brings to her work setting? Clearly, the pressures, stresses, and traumas that occur (some more subtle than others) bring about the sad-but-common transformation from bubbly neophyte to jaded professional.

Nurses in the hospital are set up to fail. Typically, they learn to accomplish a great amount of work in a very short period of time. However, regardless of the degree of work completed, someone is always quick to point out what was overlooked. Nurses do not receive a great deal of positive reinforcement. Frustration results from doing one's best and finding that only the work left undone was remarked upon.

The problem in health-care agencies is the differences in goals between management and nursing professionals that lead to major conflicts. "Inflation and fiscal constraints are forcing nurse managers to promote cost containment in the face of professional desires to maintain high quality of service, and of personal needs to maintain high quality of service, and of personal needs to protect one's own standard of living" (Levenstein, 1980, p. 47). Therefore, nurses are torn between their loyalty to their profession and their employing institution.

What are the reasons for the gap between nurses' needs and goals and those of hospital administrations? One is that hospital nursing has changed dramatically over the past several years. Due to the advent of Diagnostic-Related Groups and now Managed Care, patient stays have shortened considerably. At the same time, the sophistication and awareness of hospitalized patients have risen dramatically and, with them, a concomitant expectation for nurses to increase their knowledge of both medicine and technology.

Nurses must now utilize various types of controllers and pumps, recognize lethal arrhythmias and know their treatment, be able to "troubleshoot" respirators and other machinery, and have a good working knowledge of medicine in order to work as a team with doctors. They must be prepared to assist with complex surgical procedures, administer medications safely, understand the dietary needs of their patients, and teach their patients about their diagnoses, treatments, medications, the list seems endless.

More seriously ill patients are surviving, which has made the nurse's work even more physically taxing. It is not uncommon, for example, to find patients in their 80s and 90s with multiple organ failure being treated aggressively. An example is the patient whose lungs have failed and who is being maintained on a respirator. He now requires a tremendous number of nursing care hours, since he is unable to perform any activities of daily living himself. He must receive a bath at least daily, have his airway kept patent by suctioning, be given medications and feedings through a feeding tube to his stomach, have intravenous fluids and medications monitored continuously, be given meticulous skin care, be turned on a regular basis, and be given massage to keep his skin intact and prevent bed sores.

Well over a decade ago, an official of the Department of Health and Human Services predicted that "hospitals will be huge intensive-care units by the end of 1990s" (Aiken, 1982, p. 66). How prescient she was — that is exactly what has happened! Now, nursing in the '90s has become more stressful than ever.

The term "holistic care" means that nurses must care for *every* need of their patients: physical, psychological, emotional, psychosocial, even spiritual. Our job description includes much more than "the promotion and restoration of health, the prevention of illness, and the alleviation of suffering" (Bullough, 1983, p. 69). We are also mothers, psychologists, social workers, technicians for complex machinery, and a confidante to our patients and/or their families.

A Medical-Surgical Nurse's "Typical" Day

Because of the increased number of responsibilities and diminishing number of R.N.s, thanks to the "downsizing" policies of profit-driven, health-care institutions, nurses must function in an extremely organized manner if they hope to complete their work within an eight-or-12-hour shift. The shift usually begins with a narcotic count by two nurses, followed by report. If the shift is from 7 a.m. to 3:30 p.m., report should be finished by 7:45 a.m. Report is a detailed synopsis of each patient, including diagnosis, tests already completed and their results, exams which are planned in the immediate future, blood value results, intravenous solutions, and the current status of the patient, including any unusual occurrences, i.e., chest pain, vomiting, etc.

Then begin vital signs, which include assessing and charting the patient's temperature, pulse, respirations, and blood pressure. Bed baths usually follow, during which time the nurse evaluates the patient's skin, his lungs by auscultation, response to medications or adverse reactions, tolerance of feedings, assessment of and orientation to time, place and person, and interpretation of the cardiac monitor, if one is at the bedside.

Bed-making — yes, in spite of numerous unlicensed personnel now staffing hospitals, nurses still make beds! — is usually done at this time. It is not an easy task, particularly if the patient is bedridden and/or comatose. Many patients must be fed, usually a slow and time-consuming process. If they are fed via a nasogastric tube, the tube must be checked for placement and patency prior to placing new feeding. Other patients are fed intravenously only, and even greater care is taken with this solution (known as hyperalimentation) since these patients must be weighed daily and have their blood-sugar level checked every four-to-six hours.

Nine a.m. medications will be distributed by approximately

10:15 a.m., *if* the floor is not dangerously understaffed! Medication distribution is not a simple matter of giving out some pills. It includes maintenance of intravenous fluids at the proper rate, administering antibiotics intravenously, and giving pills orally as well as through feeding tubes. Some routine medications must be given by injection, and still others must not be given until the patient's blood pressure and pulse are known, since these vital signs must be within a certain range.

The nurse never gives medications blindly, according to physicians' orders. S/he must be aware of the effects, side effects, and contraindications of all medications, and recognize allergic reactions. S/he must also be familiar with the normal dosages of all medications, so as to question an unusual order. In addition, the nurse may spend a great deal of time paging physicians to verify their orders.

Following medication administration, certain procedures and regimens must be performed for the patients. These include tracheal suctioning, turning the immobile patient from side to side every two hours so that bedsores will not develop, massaging the skin, and performing passive exercises of the patients' joints to prevent constrictures or stiffening. Intravenous bags must be replaced before they are empty.

Patients are often unstable, and therefore the shift may be completely unpredictable in terms of the care that will be indicated. Patients may complain of chest pain. They may have difficulty breathing, exhibit heavy bleeding, require blood transfusions, or need preoperative teaching. If surgery is scheduled, the nurse must complete the chart so that the patient is cleared for surgery.

Now it is 12 noon and vital signs must be taken again for unstable patients. Twelve, one, and two-o-clock medications must be given and patients must be fed lunch. Then there are bedpans, changing incontinent patients, and notes to be written on every patient. Now, if all "goes well," the nurse *may* get a break, possibly a few minutes. Of course, this is if everything is running smoothly and the patients are stable. However, because of the larger number of elderly patients with multiple organ failure, it is rare that all patients on a medical-surgical floor are stable.

Here is a typical problem with which a nurse might be confronted. One day, while I was working as a clinical instructor, a student was completing a pre-operative checklist. We spent at least an hour straightening out all the problems, including lack of a consent for the amputation of a leg. Finally, verbal consent was obtained from the patient's daughter. However, the doctor had obtained consent for amputation of the wrong leg! Also, the chest X-ray and electrocardiogram were outdated, pre-operative urine had not been sent to the lab, and the anesthesiologist had not seen the patient.

When I told the surgeon that no consent had been signed for anesthesia, he stated that the patient would be having local anesthesia, and therefore did not need this legal form. Local anesthesia for an amputation! Not only is this type of situation frustrating and frightening, but there is no time built into the shift for handling these problems. Once these arise, the nurse may very well work through eight or nine hours straight. It is no wonder that nurses burnout.

There are also emotional stresses that sap the nurse's energy. A psychiatric-liaison nurse, Ms. Smith, recounted the following story. She was asked by staff nurses on a surgical floor to see a patient whose wife had just passed away. The nurses were upset because Mr. M.'s doctor had decided not to tell him that his wife had died and they felt he had a right to be informed. Ms. Smith finally convinced the doctor to tell his patient of his wife's death, but he refused to allow him to attend the funeral. Ms. Smith then consulted two other physicians who determined that the patient was stable enough to go the funeral. However, Mr. M.'s physician remained adamant in his decision.

Ms. Smith spoke to Mr. M. and told him of his physician's

decision, to which he replied, "If I don't go to my wife's funeral, I'll die." Ms. Smith relayed this statement to the physician, who told Ms. Smith that she was "interfering" with the care of his patient and that he would not change his mind. On the day of the funeral, Ms. Smith learned that at 12 noon, Mr. M. stood up, stated, "I should be at my wife's funeral," and dropped dead.

This story demonstrates the helplessness that nurses some-times encounter. Often, it is the result of a conflict between the wis-dom and judgment of two professionals. When those professionals are a nurse and a physician, it is the physician who almost always prevails. In discussing patients' rights, Leah Curtin states: "Although laws can protect certain aspects of human rights, there is a vast area that laws cannot protect. For example, the law can restrain me from killing you, but it cannot require me to respect your humanity, to treat you with decency, kindness, or understanding" (Curtin, 1982, p. 80).

R.N.s, as health professionals, are faced with ethical dilem-mas, such as this one, on a regular basis. All of them wear nurses down until they are finally depleted and, yes, burned-out. There are other common occurrences that also lead to anger and frustration. Lack of cooperation from ancillary personnel is one. While working one weekend in a local hospital, I was caring for a patient who needed a transfusion. His blood count had dropped dramatically from the previous day, but the blood-bank technician, asking why the patient had not been transfused during the week, was upset that I needed this unit of blood on Saturday!

Then there is the chronically inadequate supply of linen. It is unconscionable that hospitals are now "saving money" by allotting one sheet, towel, and washcloth a day for each patient, even the in-continent patient who requires much more. Nurses must then split plastic bags and use them on the beds in an attempt to save the sheet underneath. This is hardly the "professional" care nurses want to deliver. Yet, these are the conditions under which we must labor. Nurses only ask that they have adequate staffing and supplies to give their patients the kind of care they require and deserve. Today, they have neither!

Environmental Hazards that Lead to Burnout

Everyday, nurses are faced with dangerous and even life-threatening situations. How often have we been exposed to, but unaware of, patients with tuberculosis, active hepatitis, or even AIDS? It is not uncommon to care for a patient for one or even two weeks and then find out that the patient has a contagious disease. This often happens when patients — and there are many of them — are admitted to the hospital with an indefinite diagnoses, and while various diseases are being ruled out. Until a diagnosis is confirmed, no special precautions are suggested, mandated, or taken.

To me, this demonstrates the hospital's and physicians' total lack of respect and concern for the welfare of nurses. If a physician is even slightly suspicious that a patient may have a contagious disease, why not place the patient on prophylactic precautions? When I posed this question to various physicians, a common response was that nurses were being "overcautious" and "over-concerned." Also, many physicians feel that their patient will be "upset" if s/he is placed on special precautions of any kind. Well, nurses certainly appreciate a patient's right to be protected against unwarranted embarrassment or fear, but why should this concern be a one-way street?

The following is a classic case in which the welfare of nurses and other personnel was not considered. While working on a medical floor with a group of students, I assigned a very ill patient, Mr. J., to a student. Mr. J had numerous bedsores that had a foul odor, indicating to me that he was badly infected. When the doctors were confronted with the question of placing the patient on some form if isolation in order to protect him as well as his caretakers, the doctors felt it was not necessary. We took the initiative to send cultures of the patient's wounds, which proved to be very infectious. We then notified the Infectious Disease Committee, which reviewed the case and decided Mr. J. required contact isolation.

Contact isolation meant that Mr. J.'s caretakers had to wear gloves and gowns when in contact with his wounds and linen, and that his linen had to be disposed of in a special manner so that it could be laundered properly. If we had not taken the initiative to send cultures on Mr. J., we would not have taken the proper precautions and could easily have become contaminated. The physician showed no concern for the nurses in this case. This was a perfect example of NURSE ABUSE.

HIV has made traditional forms of isolation obsolete. Before the advent of this fatal, incurable virus, risk of infecting the nursing staff was held with little regard, partially because physicians believed they could cure any diseases health-care workers contracted from their patients. Once HIV's threat became known, hospital personnel were instructed to exercise "Universal Precautions," to treat all of our patients as if they had the most deadly, contagious diseases, and to take the appropriate precautions, i.e., gloves, masks, plastic aprons, etc.

Hospital administrators quickly jumped on this bandwagon, as they could now claim, if a health-care worker became ill, that it was the individual practitioner's responsibility to follow their policy on universal precautions and protect themselves from life-threatening illness. Here is yet another attempt by administration at avoiding liability or paying workman's compensation should a nurse become infected while performing her duties. There seems to be no limit to how employers wish to abandon the providers of patient care. Even the infection and death of a nurse for performing her duties has become fertile grounds for NURSE ABUSE.

Some physicians are more obvious about their lack of concern for nurses than others. A friend of mine who is a registered nurse was working in a doctor's office when a patient diagnosed with AIDS came to the office. The doctor not only asked the nurse to draw blood from the patient, but also requested an in-house complete blood count. This would have required the nurse to open the blood tube to take a sample, thereby greatly increasing her chances of becoming contaminated. Because she was aware of the risk, and even questioned the necessity of the test, she refused to draw the blood. The doctor, rather than drawing the blood himself, decided the tests were not necessary. This situation brings up some interesting questions:

1.   Was it really necessary to request blood work on this patient in the first place? Obviously, it wasn't, since the doctor changed his mind when it became his responsibility.

2.   By exposing the nurse to contaminated blood when it was not necessary, doesn't this situation demonstrate a complete lack of concern for her welfare? Again, it obviously does, since the doctor would have drawn the blood if it was imperative.

3.   How does this kind of (common) situation affect the nurse? Needless to say, the nurse was very angry and upset with the doctor. The rapport and mutual respect that may have existed prior to this incident were negatively affected.

I am not at all advocating that nurses refuse to care for patients with contagious diseases. But I believe that nurses and associated health-care workers should not be exposed to contaminated blood or other body fluids needlessly, and they should be warned so the proper precautions can be taken.

Another Cause of Burnout —
The Doctor-Nurse Relationship

Another area of NURSE ABUSE arises from the attitudes of many physicians that nurses are there to follow their orders blindly. In 1909, Beates noted that the nurse should "never attempt to appear learned and of great importance...she should be able and willing to render intelligent obedience to the instructions of the attending physician, and carry out his orders to the letter" (Ashley, 1976, p. 21). It is interesting to note that Beates made this statement in *1909!* Yet, current attitudes towards nurses are essentially the same.

There is simply no counting the many millions of lives that have been saved as a result of nurses' refusal to follow orders blindly. Any experienced nurse who has worked in a hospital in July (when the new interns arrive) knows what a fiasco this scenario is. The new doctors write orders without having any idea of appropriate medication dosages, or the untoward or antagonistic effects to other medications. The problem is so obvious to seasoned nurses and so potentially dangerous that in one hospital in which I was employed, head nurses and supervisors were asked not to take vacation in July!

Many physicians are not able to accept the fact that an experienced nurse can be a tremendous asset to his or her care of the patient. Some are offended when a nurse suggests a particular therapy or treatment. The nurse has to "tread lightly" and be very careful in the way s/he approaches the physician. Because s/he is in a subordinate position, s/he must "play a game" to obtain an order to give the patient better care. Psychiatrist Leonard Stein described nurse-physician relationships in terms of "a doctor-nurse game in which a nurse must appear to be passive. In this game, any suggestion a nurse makes to a doctor must be masked in such a way as to seem as if it were his idea, and a doctor may not openly seek advice from a nurse."

A study published in 1985 reported that the "doctor-nurse

game" described by Stein over 20-years ago is still being played. A resident interviewed for the study commented: "I have seen nurses, who really know a lot more than the intern, kind of gently guide him (the intern) into making the right decision...They make some very good decisions and make some very helpful suggestions sometimes...It is like trying to guide the ship without actually taking hold of the wheel. There are nurses who are good at that" (Prescott, 1985, p. 83). Unfortunately, we have entered yet another decade, the 1990s, with this communication style still firmly in place.

One day, while working on surgical intensive-care unit, my patient's blood count dropped to a dangerously low level. I drew a sample of blood from him and sent it to the lab so that two transfusions would be prepared. When the doctor came to the unit, I asked that he write the order for a transfusion, but he said no. I knew immediately that if I had informed him of the patient's blood count and asked him what *he* would like to do, he probably would have ordered the transfusion. This form of NURSE ABUSE can be the most degrading, since it prevents nurses from being able to act like the intelligent, educated, and clinically experienced professionals they are.

One physician summed up the problem like this: "Nursing is a very demanding profession. To start with, nurses must learn everything a doctor learns, so that whenever a situation arises that might develop into a mistake on the part of the doctor if the nurse did what the doctor ordered instead of what he meant to do, the nurse can distinguish the latter from the former and prevent the mistake from occurring. Then nurses must learn how to use this knowledge so that neither the doctor nor the patient is aware they possess it, for in the former instance, it might cause the patient to lose confidence in the doctor, and in the latter, it might cause the doctor to lose confidence in himself. Finally, if despite a nurse's best efforts things are not going well between doctor and patient, and the nurse can't patch it up, the nurse must take the blame. Nurses are very patient. They realize their reward will not be in this lifetime, for to receive even a fraction of the recognition they deserve would be to lessen the importance of the doctor. Nurses often believe in reincarnation" (Conger, 1988, p 62).

The Nurse, Ethical Decisions, and Burnout

The following concerns a graduate nurse who became involved, quite innocently, in several ethical issues while working an evening shift on a medical floor. Sad to say, it is not an unusual occurrence in health-care today.

The young nurse checked on a patient, Mr. B., and noticed that he was pale, sweating, cold, and clammy. His blood pressure was 110/40, not his normal 160/100. He did not have a fever, but his respirations were shallow and rapid. The nurse called Mr. B.'s private physician and asked him to come see his patient, but he told her to continue monitoring and call him an hour later. She did so, reporting that her patient's blood pressure had dropped to 104/40 and his breathing was still shallow and labored. The physician again told the nurses to monitor the patient and call him if there were any significant changes. A half-hour later, Mr. B. went into cardiac arrest. He was revived and transferred to the intensive-care unit.

The nurse documented what had transpired, including her communications with Mr. B.'s physician and Mr. B's family. Soon after, they all met at the hospital, where the physician told the family, "If only the nurse had called me sooner, all this could have been avoided." The family, believing the nurse had been negligent in her care, complained to the administration, which demanded that she answer the charges. She explained that she had noted the change in the patient's condition, notified the physician — not once, but twice — and documented everything in her nursing notes, which administration confirmed.

Nevertheless, the family demanded a full investigation, during which the physician denied the nurse had called him and accused her of falsifying her nursing notes. It was unlikely that the physician was being honest, since he did not report the nurse to administration for either negligent care of his patient or falsifying the records until the investigation was brought on by the family. The end result was that it was the nurse's word against the physician's (Curtin, 1982, p. 255).

This situation, a typical cause of burnout, is sad and frustrating for a number of reasons, and not particularly unusual. Nurses are often humiliated, harassed, and abused in the same way this physician humiliated, harassed, and abused this nurse. It is no wonder that dedicated nurses leave their positions and even their careers.

As Leah Curtin (1982, p. 264) stated in her analysis of this situation: "Dishonest conduct among health professionals results in distrust and fear. It undermines the basis of patient-professional relationships, damages the credibility of health-care institutions, and destroys interprofessional relationships."

Patient Advocacy and Burnout

The American Nurses Association's Code for Nurses states: "The nurse must act to safeguard the client and the public when health-care and safety are affected by the incompetent, unethical, or illegal practice of any person." Therefore, the nurse has a moral obligation and responsibility to the welfare of his or her patient. Does this not also imply that s/he has a legal responsibility to refuse to follow a doctor's order if s/he feels it is unsafe or unethical?

Since nurses are legally licensed and are not unskilled laborers who are following orders blindly, I feel they must follow orders *only* if they feel the orders are safe and will not harm the patient in any way. It is difficult to instill this concept in nursing students because many still believe that doctors are God-like and make no mistakes. Having been a nurse for many years, however, I can say with authority that doctors are human and do make mistakes, though some might argue the point. In fact, they should be thankful that nurses are educated and always present, because we serve as a checks-and-balances system that results in safer care for the patient.

While working in a local hospital, a new physician ordered a gram of lidocaine to be given to his patient for cardiac arrhythmias. It was to be given directly intravenously as a bolus or loading dose. The nurse refused to give the dose, stating that this dose of lidocaine would kill the patient. The physician then realized he needed only 1/20th of the original dose. In this case, the nurse had a legal responsibility to refuse to draw up the large dose, since her first priority was to act to safeguard the patient.

Yet many nurses suffer severe consequences, i.e., disciplinary action or even job loss, for practicing their profession responsibly. Part of the problem that exists today is that nurses are expected to give optimum and safe care while working with a minimum number of staff and inadequate supplies. We have little to no authority, yet lives are dependent upon us.

A good example concerns intensive-care nurses who refused to accept a critically ill patient to their dangerously understaffed unit because they could not guarantee him safe care. They notified the admitting physician and their supervisor of their situation and the hospital suspended them without pay! The nurses took the case to court, but the court ruled against them, saying that "nurses are to obey first, and grieve later." The judgment demonstrated to the nurses that they were seen only as employees by the court and the hospital, and that they "must do as they are told" (Wilson, 1987, p. 21).

Death-and-Dying and Burnout

Another complex subject, one which involves emotional, legal, and ethical issues, concerns patients who are irreversibly dying. Part of the problem is that many hospitals do not have a clear-cut policy regarding patients who have no hope of surviving. The other part of the problem is the reluctance of physicians to write a "Do Not Resuscitate" order. Because of this ambivalence, nurses are often caught between the patient's and/or family's wishes for no extraordinary measures to be taken, and the wishes of the physician to do everything possible for the patient.

According to Leah Curtin (1982, p. 300): "As a rule, irreversibly dying patients should not be subjected to cardiopulmonary resuscitation. Pragmatically speaking, it achieves nothing. All that results is more agony for the dying and lasting scars for the living. It is a degrading and unnecessary interruption of a person's dying."

While family and patients have their own feelings to contend with, nurses are actually caring for these patients. It is frustrating to care for patients whom we know will not benefit from our care, but require a tremendous number of nursing hours, precious hours that could be spent with patients who could benefit from our care. This may sound cold and calculating, but the truth is that choices must constantly be made as to whom will receive transplants, time on dialysis machines, the list goes on.

If a clear-cut order is not written, or a decision is not made, the nurse is then placed in the position of having to resuscitate a patient s/he may believe should be allowed to die naturally. Often the verbal decisions of the patient or family conflict with written orders, leaving nurses in a precarious and uncomfortable position. Nurses sometimes make a decision to run a "Slow Code," and an excessive amount of time elapses before cardio-pulmonary resuscitation is begun. In this way, nurses can officially say the patient was "coded," knowing that the code might not succeed.

This is not a legal course of action and nurses are liable if they take it. To avoid such a situation, the decision to resuscitate or not must be discussed with the appropriate persons and decided *prior to* the event of death. I have been involved with many cardiac arrests where there was a doubt as to whether the patient should be resuscitated, and CPR was in progress while someone was attempting to contact the patient's physician.

When physicians disagree, it can result in chaos for the nurses caring for the involved patient. A student nurse was assigned to a patient who was not to be resuscitated. The resident, who had first spoken to the family, had written the order "Do Not Resuscitate." On checking the orders later that morning, I discovered that the private physician had drawn a line through the order, and written "Error" over it. The student rightfully believed that the family had changed their minds, and the patient was to be resuscitated in the event of cardiac arrest. However, the private physician had indicated in his progress notes that he still did not want the patient to be resuscitated. Yet, he did not want the order *written.*

After removing the student from the case, and informing the head nurse of the dilemma, we hoped the patient would not experience a cardiac arrest while we were obtaining a proper order. Eventually the private physician rewrote the order not to resuscitate. If the patient had arrested, we would have had to perform CPR, knowing that this was against the wishes of the family. It is unfair and unethical that nurses are placed in these compromising positions.

Other heart-wrenching situations occur frequently, placing the nurse in a difficult position. One of the most difficult is when a patient is alert and oriented, but dying from a terminal disease. Mr. R. was dying from lung cancer and respirator-dependent. He was extremely uncomfortable, literally drowning in his own fluids, and he continually attempted to disconnect himself from the respirator so he would die. The staff was forced to restrain his hands, but he kept begging to be put out of his misery. Morally, the staff could do nothing. I found myself avoiding his room and hoping his death would come quickly. He finally did pass away, but the effect on the nursing staff was devastating. Situations like this are the true "reality shock" for nurses.

Nursing Salaries and Burnout

Based on the degree of education acquired by nurses, as well as the ethical, moral, and legal situations in which they are placed, it is clear that nursing salaries should be exceptional compared to other, related professions. However, they are not.

Given the decreased hospital occupancy rates and the increased number of nurses in the past three decades, why is there such a shortage of nurses in our hospitals? One explanation is related to wages of nurses. We've been looking at the many stressful situations in which nurses are placed, yet nurses' incomes are not comparable with those of other occupations predominantly filled by women in significantly less-responsible and stressful jobs.

Indeed, the numbers of nurses in hospitals increased as wages did, peaking in 1992. However, there still existed a gap in staffing because of the increase in patient acuity. Patients were no longer admitted to hospitals unless they were extremely ill. But, long before nursing and patient-care needs reached parity, the pendulum swung the other way and administrators began to layoff R.N.s to maximize their profits.

These administrators, fiercely guarding their own positions, have, in fact, increased the number of management positions. Today, there are two hospital administrators for each in-patient bed, whether that bed is occupied or not! A hospitalized patient, in the mid-'90s, can have his or her own personal "billing executive," but not the care of a registered nurse to provide bedside care. The nursing shortage is still with us, but nurses continue to be devalued and are now occupying unemployment lines instead of hospitals.

When we look at all of the stresses affecting nurses, it is no wonder that so many burn out. I believe a cycle has started that may be impossible to break. The cycle began when nurses left hospitals because of low salaries, poor working conditions, and lack of respect from administration and physicians. Today, hospitals are sacrificing patient care to huge corporate profits by replacing R.N.s with unlicensed aides, compelling the few remaining R.N.s to supervise unwieldy staffs, do mandatory overtime, and float to areas outside their expertise. This is the ultimate in NURSE ABUSE.

Yes, there are many forms of NURSE ABUSE. Most nurses join the professional because of an innate desire to help people, and they gain a great deal of satisfaction from it. But in order to function professionally and competently, nurses themselves must have their basic needs met. Those needs include adequate supplies, a feasible nurse-patient ratio, salaries that compensate for clinical expertise, education, and the level of care rendered, and respect for who we are and what we do.

If physicians and hospitals would treat nurses with the respect they deserve, supply adequate staffing, and pay decent salaries, many of the abuses that nurses experience would dissipate, and NURSE ABUSE would be resolved. However, it is clear, at least for the present, that profits are more important than patient care, and definitely more important than dignified treatment of the caretakers.

References

Aiken, L. (ed). (1982). *Nursing in the 1980s: Crises, Opportunities, Challenges.* J.B. Lippincott Co. Philadelphia.

American Hospital Association. (1980). Hospital Statistics. Chicago: American Hospital Association.

American Nurses Association's Code for Nurses with Interpretive Statements. (1976). American Nurses Association, Kansas City, Missouri.

Ashley, J. (1976). *Hospitals, Paternalism, and the Role of the Nurse.* New York: Teacher's College, Columbia University Press.

Bullough B., Bullough V., and Soukup M.C. (1983). *Nursing Issues and Nursing Strategies for the 1980s.* Springer Publishing Company, New York.

Cherniss, C. (1987). Professional Burnout in Human Service Organizations. New York, Praeger, 1980, as quoted in *Nursing Times*, 1987, Aug. 12-18; 83 (32) 55-57.

Conger, B. (1988). *Bag Balm and Dust Tape: Tales of a Vermont Doctor.* Little, Brown & Company.

Curtin L., & Flaherty M.J. (1982). *Nursing Ethics: Theories and Pragmatics.* Brady Communications Company, Inc.

Firth, H. McIntee J., McKeown P., & Britton P. (1986). Burnout and Professional Depression: Related Concepts. *Journal of Advanced Nursing*, 11(6), p. 634.

Levenstein, A. (1980). The Adversaries. *Supervisor Nurse*, 2, 47.

Prescott P.A. and Bowen S. (1985). Physician-Nurse Relationship. *Annals of Internal Medicine*, 103 (July) 12, as quoted in *Ethics in Nursing*.

U.S. Bureau of the Census. (1980). Statistical Abstract of the United States. Washington D.C.: U.S. Bureau of the Census.

Wilson, J. (1987). Why Nurses Leave Nursing. *The Canadian Nurse*. March, 21-23.

Chapter Five

LABOR LAW AND NURSE ABUSE: IS THERE LEGAL PROTECTION FOR NURSES?

by Harold Stearley, R.N., B.S.N., CCRN

Nurse abuse takes many diverse forms in institutional and public settings. Yet most of it goes unchecked. Why is it that nurses seem so powerless to fight back against the sweat-shop mentality imposed on them by hospital and nursing administrators?

It's because, for the most part, nurses have been convinced that labor-law protection is not good for them. By simple brain-washing techniques, management has effectively convinced them that to be a "professional," one must not act like management's definition of a blue-collar laborer.

While nurses continue to be mistreated and abused as common laborers, they are told that to complain, to organize, to grieve, to protest, to bargain collectively, or to contract independently are all trade-marks of laborers, not professionals. It often seems that bricklayers and pipe-fitters have more labor-law protection than nurses, simply because these workers have learned how to use existing laws to protect themselves against exploitation.

Nurses are told they must "buck-up" when they are short-staffed and working in dangerous environments. They are told they must work mandatory over-time, and they then have their hours manipulated to prevent them from earning overtime wages. How? They are classified as part-time to prevent them from earning benefit packages. They are also told that staying past one's shift to catch up or chart cannot be placed on time sheets.

Management cares not if nurses are unable to take a meal break or have never made it to the restroom during their grueling shifts. And, when a lawsuit charges that nurses were unable to provide appropriate care, management simply walks away and leaves nurses' licenses hanging in the breeze.

Despite all this, many of our colleagues still delude themselves into believing management is somehow on their side, doing what is best for them. It often takes a negative personal experience to shake nurses out of this delusion, but all too often it is too late to fight back.

My own shock came when, as the charge nurse on a busy surgical unit, I was named in a lawsuit when a patient coded and, subsequently, remained in a persistent vegetative state. All the nurses I was working with that night were named in the lawsuit. It was not uncommon on my unit for me to be the only licensed person, with most of the rest of the staff composed of graduate nurses. Despite my continued objections, I had been told the conditions were "safe."

The attorney who represented the institution reached an out-of-court settlement. But the hospital simply walked away from the nurses, offering no support or protection. Fortunately, the State Board of Nursing took no additional action against my license, but the entire experience was humiliating.

However, the event opened my eyes to a system that routinely exploits nurses for financial gain at all costs, including sacrificing patients and nursing licenses. I learned the value of becoming proactive and striking before I was again victimized. I learned that if nurses are truly going to call themselves professionals, they must take control of their profession, become familiar with labor law, and seize every opportunity to fight for their rights as professionals.

Retaliatory Termination

A 20-year veteran of nursing, Peter Ramme, R.N., CEN, CCRN, worked for a California hospital's Emergency Department for six-and-a-half years with an exemplary record. But when he became affiliated with the California Nurses Association, he began to speak out on nursing issues, openly confronting the Vice President of Nursing about preserving overtime wages for staff nurses who worked 12-hour shifts.

The director of his ED perceived Mr. Ramme as a threat to management. Determined to terminate his employment, she made him a target of NURSE ABUSE. First, the director took issue with Mr. Ramme's use of a computer, which he used only during his breaks. However, Mr. Ramme filed a grievance about this action and won his point.

Next, Mr. Ramme, responding to a great number of malicious phone calls to the ED, contacted the hospital's communications supervisor, security, and nursing management, but received no support. He and the ED staff then resorted to calling the police, who traced the calls and arrested the perpetrator.

Subsequent to this episode, Mr. Ramme filed statements of concern with Quality Assurance and grievances with his supervisors in order to gain future security — and less interference with patient care — for the ED staff. He was given a two-day suspension for "insubordination."

One day, Mr. Ramme, the most experienced nurse on duty, attended an overdose patient by administering activated charcoal, making sure vital signs were stable and pulse oximetry was within normal parameters, protecting the patient's airway, and putting the cardiac monitor in place, with alarms activated. When the physician ordered necessary equipment, Mr. Ramme went to get it, leaving the patient in the care of a medical resident.

Upon his return, the emergency physician and the ED's director complained about the patient being left "unattended." Mr. Ramme informed the doctor that he *was* attending the patient and continued his care. Finally, he transferred the patient, in stable condition, to the intensive-care unit, as ordered. But within 36 hours, Mr. Ramme was notified he was suspended indefinitely, pending an investigation into the "incident."

Subsequently, he was terminated for "serious neglect" and "inconsistent, inadequate, and inappropriate documentation with incorrect punctuation." The patient in question suffered no harm, and Mr. Ramme maintained no neglect occurred.

Unfortunately for Mr. Ramme, no attorney was willing to take his case of retaliatory termination to court without first being paid a large fee. Many managers exploit the fact that nurses like Mr. Ramme simply cannot afford to fight back, and freely violate their employment rights knowing they can get away with such abuse.

Learn Your Rights and Keep Your Job

For nurses to become effective fighters for their own rights, they must know what those rights are. In most states, nurses' employment status is classified as "at will." Unless your state law holds exception to this doctrine, or you are a union member or have your own employment contract, then you are subject to dismissal any time, without cause, "at will" of your employer. This archaic concept from English Common Law is, to this day, a point of contention between labor and management.

Management claims this doctrine is fair since it allows employees to terminate their employment "at will." Of course, it also gives management the ability to fire nurses "at will." Some equality! Leaving a position by choice is not comparable to being fired for no reason at all!

Over time, and as a result of many lawsuits, this doctrine has been amended to protect the public's interests. Obviously, if management were able to fire anyone without justification, the potential for exploiting employees would have no limits. Today, four exceptions to the "at will" doctrine are recognized: Public Policy, Good Faith, Contract, and Wrongful Termination.

Public Policy is invoked when issues of discrimination arise. Employees cannot be discriminated against based on race, sex, age, religion, or national origin. Further, an employer cannot terminate anyone who performs jury duty, or gives testimony at trials or hearings.

Good Faith comes into play when employers try to terminate an individual out of bad faith or malice. In one instance in Massachusetts, an employer unsuccessfully attempted to terminate a salesman to avoid paying his agreed-upon commission.

Wrongful Termination recognizes that employees are sometimes required to perform a public duty that conflicts with their employers, for instance, reporting dangerous practices at a nuclear power plant. The courts created a category called "whistle blowers" to identify employees who perform beneficial service to the public. Nurses who report unsafe or negligent practices fall into this category.

Employment contracts, whether explicit or implied, guarantee that both parties live up to the terms of employment. In the early days of unionization, employers tried to sidestep contracts by offering their employees benefits and personnel policies in exchange for union contracts. To the surprise of many employers, some courts held these policies and procedures to be employment contracts which, effectively, provided employees a defense against termination "at will." In essence, the roots of modern-day benefit packages derived, not from employers wanting to benefit their employees, but from their desire to bust unions and dilute the power of employees.

Fortunately, many nurses are informed of their rights and have taken their grievances into the courtroom. However, not all of these cases had satisfactory outcomes. Nevertheless, the fight is often more important than the outcome. Over time, precedent is set that serves to defend other nurses from abuse.

Fighting Back

In the case Havens vs. Tomball Community Hospital - 793 S. W. 2d 690 (1990), the head nurse of a labor-and-delivery unit protested a physician's decision to administer epidural anesthesia on a mother in labor, and then leave the hospital. The physician was not authorized by the hospital to perform the procedure, and his subsequent absence made the nurse feel the life of the mother and infant were in jeopardy. The nurse's reward for her concern was harassment from the physician and the director of nursing, followed by her termination.

The 215th District Court granted summary judgment in favor of the hospital regarding the nurse's claims of retaliatory discharge. The Court of Appeals, First District, reversed the judgment of the lower court in favor of the nurse, citing "intentional infliction of emotional distress" stemming from the behavior of the above-mentioned parties. In Texas, this is a separate cause of action, so the nurse won because of the infliction of emotional distress, instead of the true cause of action, retaliatory termination. (Tammelleo, 1990, p. 3).

In Kirk vs. Mercy Hospital Tri-County, 851 S. W. 2d 617 - Mo. (1993), a patient in a Missouri hospital died from toxic-shock syndrome. The nurse on the case had sought treatment for the patient, and protested when none was provided. She was terminated for "not staying out of it." The Circuit Court of Wright County granted summary judgment for the hospital, stating that the public policy exception to the employment-at-will doctrine did not apply to this case. However, the Missouri Court of Appeals ruled that the public-policy issue did exist relative to Missouri's State Nursing Practice Act, which requires nurses to pursue the best possible care for their patients.

The Court also noted that the nurse could have faced disciplinary action from the State Board of Nursing had she ignored the improper treatment her patient had received. The administration's instructions for her to "stay out of it" were not only inappropriate, but placed the nurse in the position of breaking the law. (Missouri Reports, 1993).

In another case, the outcome for a nurse was not so favorable. In Wright vs. Shriners Hospital - 589 N. E. 2d 1241 - MA (1992), an assistant director of nursing was terminated for revealing that inconsistent practices and procedures were jeopardizing patient care. The hospital administrators were upset that an internal audit was scheduled to be repeated to reexamine patient-care issues, and they fired the ADN. A jury trial ruled in favor of the nurse, but upon appeal, the Supreme Judicial Court of Massachusetts reversed the lower court's judgment, stating that not enough evidence was presented to show that public policy had been violated. (Tammelleo, 1992, p. 2).

Clearly, this presents a quandary for nurses who are faced with flagrant abuses and malpractice in the patient-care arena. Employers want nurses to be quiet, and they benefit from "at will doctrines" because they can fire nurses who threaten the status quo, or for no reason at all. It is easy to see why so many nurses remain quiet in the face of negligent medical practice. Yet it is our duty to protect patients. We've been quiet too long!

If you are a victim of abusive termination tactics, it will not be easy to continue your employment elsewhere. Interactions with vindictive managers often come back to haunt you. Here are some ways to go about bringing a grievance to public awareness — or to the courtroom.

1.   Become informed about your rights, and when they are being violated.

2.   Document every detail of any negligent event in a separate employment journal, not in a personal journal. Data from a

personal journal may end up in court along with employment data.

3.   Seek the advice of an attorney who has expertise in your kind of case.

4.   Lobby Congress for a special provision, or amendment, to the "at will" doctrine that will protect employees from malicious persecution vis-a-vis patient-care issues.

5.   Institute a legal-defense fund for nurses who are unable to afford the cost of defending themselves in court.

Workman's Compensation

No issue is of greater concern to nurses than being physically injured on the job. Many nurses, however, are not familiar with existing laws and how they might benefit from them, so they neglect taking action. Even workman's compensation can victimize nurses. A thorough understanding of the regulations that relate to employees' injuries is necessary, especially today when cutbacks in staff are bringing about increased on-the-job injuries and accidents.

In Minnesota, for example, injuries increased substantially as the number of nurses represented in bargaining units decreased. R.N. bargaining-unit positions dropped from 7,367 in 1990 to 6712 in 1994, while the number of injuries rose 6.35 percent to 11.75 percent (Himali, 1995, p. 19).

These statistics should not be surprising. With increased workloads and fewer staff, exhausted nurses are less vigilant about the hospital's inherent hazards. This is not helped by the fact that nursing managers go to great lengths to minimize claims for workman's compensation, often telling employees they are not eligible. Unfortunately, many nurses believe what they are told, and so fail to pursue legitimate complaints.

Compensation is not reserved for back injuries. At least this is what the Court of Appeals of Oklahoma determined when Vera James, L.P.N., went to pick up her paycheck at St. Anthony Hospital on her day off and fell down at the entrance of the institution, sustaining a fracture. The court held that James' injury arose out of her employment because being paid is a major benchmark of the employer-employee relationship (Oklahoma Reports, 1994).

What happens when you're injured in an automobile while driving to or from work? Generally, an employer is not liable for injuries sustained off the premises of employment. However, in the case of agency nurses, this law has exceptions. JoAnn Peterson, L.P.N., was driving to her assigned workplace when she had an auto accident and sustained a fracture. Her case was appealed to the Supreme Court of Pennsylvania, which determined she was "furthering the business of the agency" and awarded her compensation (Pennsylvania Reports, 1991).

In another auto-related case, Theresa Facey, a nursing assistant for Geriatric and Medical Centers in Pennsylvania, sprained her lumbar spine in a company van that was taking her to work. In Pennsylvania, a "Ridesharing Act" excludes payment of compensation when injured in such circumstance, but in this case the employer granted compensation for two years prior to challenging it. The court determined the employer had not investigated the facts of the accident prior to providing compensation and was therefore liable to continue payments (Tammelleo, 1994, p. 3).

What if you are injured when not taking care of patients? While on the job, Sue Pansegrau, R.N., lost consciousness, fell to the floor, and received a skull fracture and brain stem injury. Compensation was originally awarded until the insurance carrier, National Union Fire Insurance Company of Pittsburgh, filed suit to deny her benefits in the U. S. District Court for the Northern District of Texas.

The district court ruled in Ms. Pansegrau's favor, but also ruled she was unable to receive total compensation for bills paid by her medical insurance. Ms. Pansegrau appealed to the U. S. Court of Appeals, Fifth Circuit, and was subsequently awarded full damages

(Texas Reports, 1994). Nurses take note! You are entitled to recover the full value of compensation, even if another insurance carrier has provided some payment.

In another case, Patricia Herman, R.N. died of a heart attack on the job. Miner's Hospital, in New Mexico, was obligated by the Worker's Compensation Act to file a "first report of accident," but failed to do so, claiming the injury was not work related. Ms. Herman's husband, pursuing the case all the way to the state's Supreme Court, won on the grounds that her stressful occupation could have caused the heart attack (New Mexico Reports, 1991).

Finally, a look at a major limitation of Workman's Compensation. On November 13, 1986, Jenera Mundy, R.N., reported to Charity Hospital near her Louisiana home, where an assailant entered her elevator and stabbed her in the neck, chest, back, arms, and hands. Her case was covered by workman's compensation, but once recovered from her injuries, she was afraid to return to work at the same institution. (No security guards had been present the night of her assault.)

Ms. Mundy accepted a lower-paying position elsewhere and filed suit against Charity Hospital for "failure to maintain a reasonably safe environment for its employees, and failing to provide adequate security." The court ruled this was strictly a workman's compensation issue, and Mundy was unable to recover any additional damages, despite her additional loss of income and the emotional injuries she had sustained (Louisiana Reports, 1991).

As you can see some protection and compensation is available to nurses. In other cases, however, nurses' ability to recover damages is limited, clearly another example of NURSE ABUSE.

Discrimination

Discrimination can take all sorts of shapes and forms: age, gender, pregnancy, religious beliefs, sexual preferences, disabilities—you name it and people will discriminate against it. But people also fight discrimination, which accounts for the fact that the last decades have seen the enaction of many anti-discrimination laws: the 1964 Civil Rights Act, the 1967 Age Discrimination in Employment Act, the 1978 Pregnancy Discrimination Act, and the 1990 Americans with Disabilities Act (ADA) (Calfee, 1996, p. 35). All were passed to protect workers from the ruthless tactics of their employers.

But discrimination still permeates our society, and, even in the late 1990s, discrimination against nurses is widespread and commonplace.

Edna Ruth Harris filed a charge with the Equal Employment Opportunity Commission claiming Presbyterian/Saint Luke's Medical Center in Colorado had discriminated against her when levying a three-day suspension for racist behavior. Her supervisor retaliated by filing complaints against her with the State Board of Nursing.

The U. S. District Court in Colorado ruled against nurse Harris, saying she should have asserted her claim under Title VII of the 1964 Civil Rights Act, not under another provision her attorney chose to argue (Colorado Reports, 1991). This case makes it clear that nurses not only have to know the law, they must also choose their attorneys wisely.

Even the correct legal strategy can fail in some cases. When Hilda Pappas, R.N. applied for health insurance for her family, her employer, Bethesda Hospital in Ohio, denied her coverage because her husband had heart disease and her son was confined to a wheel chair. The court ruled, however, that the ADA allows for "public accommodation," not health insurance. There is no mandate that health-care constitutes "physical use" of a place of public accommodation (Ohio Reports, 1994). This seemingly clear-cut case was suddenly upended by the fine reading and interpretation of the Act.

Can a nurse recover damages if s/he determines, years after the fact, that discrimination took place? In Little Forest Medical Center of Akron vs. Ohio Civil Rights Commission, 631 N.E. 2d 1068, a nursing assistant was able to prove his facility would not hire him because he was male. The suit was filed five years after the discrimination was discovered. Once sued, the institution offered him a job, but the court ordered the medical center to pay wages the NA would have earned during the five years (Calfee, 1996, p. 37).

As you can see, the courts will not tolerate many types of abuse, as long as the plaintiff proves his or her case. This reinforces the necessity to be on guard and maintain a workplace journal.

Sexual Harassment

In 1995, nearly 16,000 claims for sexual harassment were filed with the Equal Employment Opportunity Commission. From 46-to-72 percent of hospital-based nurses reported being subjected to this type of abuse (Wolfe, 1996,p. 61). There are several interpretations of sexual abuse, but in 1992, the U. S. Supreme Court handed down a ruling that made it easier for women to prove their cases.

Teresa Harris, was a manager at Forklift Systems, Inc., in Tennessee, and Charles Hardy was the company's president. Often, in front of other employees, Hardy made derogatory remarks towards Ms. Harris: "You're a woman, what do you know?" "We need a man as the rental manager." "You're a dumb ass woman." He also suggested they "go to the Holiday Inn to negotiate your raise." Ms. Harris quit her job and filed suit in the U.S. District Court for the Middle District of Tennessee.

In a controversial ruling, the judge found that Hardy's behavior did not create an abusive environment, but that his comments "would offend a reasonable woman, but were not so severe as to be expected to seriously affect Harris's psychological well being." The court of Appeals affirmed this decision, so Ms. Harris appealed the case to the U.S. Supreme Court, which handed down the most important ruling on this issue to date.

The court clarified the fact that sexual harassment was an unlawful employment practice, adding, "It is not limited to economic or tangible discrimination." The intent of the law, the court said, is "to strike at the entire spectrum of disparate treatment of men and women in employment." Justice Sandra Day O'Connor wrote: "When the workplace is permeated with discriminatory intimidation, ridicule, and insult that is sufficiently severe or pervasive to alter the conditions of the victim's employment and create an abusive working environment, Title VII (of the Civil Rights Act) is violated" (Tennessee Reports, 1992).

Nurses around this country should capitalize on this important legal clarification to ensure they are not sexually exploited in the institutions in which they are employed. This is one form of NURSE ABUSE nurses don't have to take anymore!

Wages and Differentials

The Fair Labor Standards Act (FLSA), and the Equal Pay Act (EPA) of 1963 were passed to outline how wages and overtime are to be paid. Areas of dispute have arisen over whether overtime is paid on seven or 14 day pay periods for time spent charting after a shift is completed, and for working during times allotted for meals and breaks.

Nurses must check with their institutions to see which schedule is used to calculate overtime. Any questions should be directed to the U. S Department of Labor, Wage and Hour Division. Do not hesitate to call to explore your rights as an employee!

There is also controversy over the "clinical ladders" institutions use, supposedly to recognize staff nurses for their achievements.

In reality, this may be just another form of exploitation. Most clinical ladders involve giving an employee a raise in salary for meeting specific goals and completing numerous extra-curricular activities. A Staff Nurse III must complete four in-service courses, two journal reviews and presentations, assist with a hospital research project, precept X number of other staff nurses, obtain X number of continuing-education units, mop the floor, clean the windows...you get my drift.

Problems with clinical ladders arise when nurses total up the time these activities take and realize how many hours they've spent working for the institution for *no* compensation. I totaled up the hours I had spent and figured I actually had taken a pay cut of $1.34 an hour!

Hospitals say they don't have to pay nurses for these hours because the clinical ladder program is voluntary. But once a nurse signs on with the ladder, the work becomes mandatory. So, which is it, voluntary or mandatory? According to federal labor law, it doesn't matter; the hospital must compensate the nurse for *any* work benefitting the employer. (The Fair Labor Standards Act of 1938 as Amended, Sections 785.7 through 785.13.)

Mixed Employment Issues — The Battles That Await Us

As long as nurses work for employers and are not independent contractors, there will be exploitation and abuse when it comes to issues of job security, floating, shift differentials, and mandatory overtime. If an employee doesn't have a written contract, management will seize every available opportunity to practice NURSE ABUSE!

Nurses can win these battles if they unite and stand their ground. Many have blazed the trail already by taking their cases to court and receiving favorable judgments that help protect all nurses.

The following court cases are particularly important, for they may help lay the foundation to resist the market forces that are dictating that registered nurses be replaced with unlicensed personnel.

In Winkleman vs. Beloit Memorial Hospital in Wisconsin, Betty Winkelman, R.N., a maternity nurse, refused to float to a unit of post-operative and geriatric patients because she felt her lack of expertise in this area might put patients at risk. She was told to find another nurse to take her place or to take an unexcused absence day and go home. Nurse Winkleman went home. The hospital then terminated her, stating that her actions constituted "a voluntary resignation." She sued for wrongful discharge and the Circuit Court of Rock County, Wisconsin, ruled in her favor.

The hospital appealed to the Supreme Court of Wisconsin, which ruled that the nurse had identified the fundamental concept of "public policy" that "provides that only qualified nurses are allowed to render services, and that nurses rendering services for which they are not qualified are subjected to sanctions under the law" (Wisconsin Reports, 1992). Further, the ruling stated "that the sick should be given care only by those who are in fact qualified to do so."

While this case involved the issue of nurses floating from unit to unit, it also applies to our present situation, nurses being replaced by UAP. Ironically, Winkelman's case occurred in 1965. Yet its ruling is extremely relevant in today's atmosphere of eliminating R.N.s.

In Darling vs. Charleston Hospital, Dorrence Darling proved that the hospital failed to maintain an adequate number of trained nurses to monitor a patient's condition, a broken leg from playing football. The patient's cast had been applied inappropriately and was too tight, but despite repeated attempts to get medical attention, he lost the leg due to gangrene.

The court rule that the hospital "Failed to have a sufficient number of trained nurses for bedside care, of all patients at all times, capable of recognizing the progressive gangrenous condition of the plaintiff's right leg, and of bringing the same to the attention of the hospital administration and to the medical staff so that adequate consultation could have been secured and such conditions rectified" (Illinois Reports, 1965).

It is clear that the lack of registered, professional nurses results in increased morbidity and mortality. Legal precedent has been set, and it may be the courts who will have to reverse the current market trends which are dismantling our profession.

Now it's our job, the job of nurses everywhere, to prove to the public, the courts, and our employers that nursing is a job for nurses, not unlicensed assistive personnel! It is the job of each and every nurse to set additional precedent to support all nurses in the struggle against NURSE ABUSE!

Legislative Update

When the National Labor Relations Act first passed over 50 years ago, it allowed supervisory personnel to participate in collective bargaining and negotiate with their employers. Employers complained that not only did they have to deal with their regular employees, but that an unfair imbalance existed between labor and management when supervisors were allowed to organize.

In 1947, after many lobbying efforts, management won, and the NLRA was amended to exclude supervisory personnel from being defined as employees (29 U.S.C., Section 152(#). Congress defined supervisors as people representing the employer with regard to hiring, transferring, discharging, promoting, disciplining, directing, etc.

In 1993, four L.P.N.s from Heartland Nursing Home in Urbana, Ohio, filed a complaint with the National Labor Relations Board regarding what they considered unfair discipline practices. The nurses had complained of deplorable working conditions, and were rewarded with termination, a familiar theme to some nurses. Heartland's

Board of Directors contended that since the nurses participated in such activities as staffing, directing unlicensed assistive personnel, evaluations, and counseling, that the L.P.N.s were supervisors and not employees, thus not protected under the NLRA.

The Administrative Law Judge reviewing the case stated that the nurses represented the interests of patients, not those of the employers, and ruled in their favor. However, the U. S. Court of Appeals, Sixth District, reversed the lower decision, stating that the test for supervisor status was inconsistent with the statute. The Appellate Court then filed for a review by the Supreme Court, which was granted. The Supreme Court, on May 23, 1994, stated that it was a false dichotomy to say that the nurses were serving the interests of the patients and not the corporation.

This judgment was a major blow to nurses seeking legal protection from NURSE ABUSE, especially at a time when management is forcing R.N.s to direct and supervise the actions of more and more UAP! In essence, it means that *any* nurse who uses independent judgment to direct the actions of any other employee — i.e., excuse me, Mr. Janitor, will you please empty the trash? — is a supervisor, and not eligible for protection under the NLRA.

However, two recent court rulings have begun to recapture labor-law protection for nurses. The Service Employees International Union won cases for R.N.s in Providence Hospital in Anchorage, Alaska, and L.P.N.s at a nursing home in Lake Katrine, New York. The court stated: "Nurses, including charge nurses, are *not* supervisors simply because they use professional judgment to direct or assign others." However, the American Hospital Association fought hard against these rulings and won a provision in which all unionizing attempts would have to be evaluated on a case-by-case basis.

Clearly, the powers-that-be want to keep nurses from uniting and organizing. After all, they have a lot at stake. If nurses continue to win their rights in court battles, management will have to treat them with the respect they deserve, and provide them with appropriate wages, benefits, and working environments.

Many battles lie ahead. Get involved, fight for yourself, and support your fellow nurses!

References

Calfee, B. E. (1996). Labor Laws: Working To Protect You. *Nursing 96*, 26(2), 34-39.

Colorado Reports.(1991). Harris v. Presbyterian/Saint Luke's Medical Center-758 F. Supp. 636.

Himali, U. (1995). An Unsafe Equation: Fewer R.N.s Equal More Workplace Injuries. *The American Nurse*, 27(5), 19.

Illinois Reports. (1965). Darling v. Charleston Hospital, 33 Ill., 2d 326. Iowa Reports. (1993). Edmunds v. Mercy Hospital, Cedar Rapids-503, N.W. 2d 877.

Louisiana Reports. (1991). Mundy v. Department of Health and Human Services. Res-580 So. 2d 493.

Missouri Reports. (1993). Kirk v. Mercy Hospital Tri-county 851 S.W. 2d 617.

New Mexico Reports. (1991). Herman v. Miner's Hospital-807 P. 2d, 734.

Ohio Reports. (1994). Pappas v. Bethesda Hospital Association-861 F. Supp. 616.

Oklahoma Reports. (1994). St. Anthony Hospital v. James-899 P. 2d 1279.

Pennsylvania Reports. (1991). Peterson v. W.C.A.B. (PRN Nursing)-597 A. 2d 1116.

Tennessee Reports. (1992). Harris v. Forklift Systems, Incorporated 114 S. Ct. 2d 367.

Texas Reports. (1994). Pansegrau v. National Union Fire Insurance Company-23 F. 3d 960.

Tammelleo, A. D. (ed.) (1990). Texas Nurse Challenges Doctor: Retaliatory Discharge. *The Regan Report on Nursing Law*, 31(10), 3.

Tammelleo, A. D. (ed.) (1992). Nurse Blows Whistle: Retaliatory Termination? *The Regan Report on Nursing Law*, 33(2), 2.

Tammelleo, A. D. (ed.) (1994). Nursing Assistant Injured In Employer's Vehicle: Workers' Compensation Coverage Issue. *The Regan Report on Nursing Law*, 35(7), 3.

The Fair Labor Standards Act of 1938, As Amended. Interpretative Bulletin, Part 785: Hours Worked. U.S. Department of Labor Wage and Hour Division.

Wisconsin Reports. (1992). Winkleman Versus Beloit Memorial Hospital, 483 N. W. 2d 211.

Wolfe, S. (1996). If You're Sexually Harassed. *RN*, February, pp. 61-64.

Chapter Six

THE PSYCHOLOGY OF ABUSE

by Joan Swirsky, R.N., M.S., CS, ACCE

"The nature of women's oppression is unique: women are oppressed as women, regardless of class or race; some women have access to wealth, but that wealth does not signify power; women are to be found everywhere, but own or control no appreciable territory;...women have little sense of dignity or self-respect or strength, since those qualities are directly related to a sense of manhood. When...women find the courage to defend themselves, to take a stand against...abuse, they are violating every notion of womanhood they have ever been taught."

Machiavelli, 1513.

Now, what exactly are we talking about when we use the term "NURSE ABUSE"? Is it similar to child abuse? On the surface, it appears different. After all, doesn't child abuse have physical manifestations — bruised little bodies, broken bones, contusions, scratches, cigarette burns? And don't the victims of child abuse have a psychological profile as well: lack of self-confidence, distrust of adults, a facility with lying (the better to cover their abusers' tracks), trouble socializing, poor school performance, a sad-eyed look? No, clearly NURSE ABUSE is not akin to child abuse.

Well, then, is it similar to wife (and woman) abuse? Again, it *seems* not to be. After all, don't wives who are abused also show the physical ravages of that abuse? Broken teeth, bruises (which they conceal with makeup, glasses and clothing), shattered bones (which they attribute to an unfortunate fall), clumps of missing hair), the list goes on. And don't they, too, have a psychological profile: oceans of self-contempt, addictive behavior, denial, depression? No, certainly NURSE ABUSE is unlike wife abuse.

But, NURSE ABUSE is, indeed, abuse, only its signs and symptoms, while more subtle, are equally insidious. Nurses may not bear the typical physical scars that characterize abused children and women, although, increasingly, physical abuse has entered the clinical arena via out-of-control patients and physicians. And nurses may not have the recognizable personality traits of other abused populations, such as the apologetic manner, the frightened demeanor, the defensive posture.

And yet, in their daily professional lives, the registered nurses of whom we are speaking are subjected to all of the mistreatments, harshness, inequities, and debasement of other abused groups. And so, the question before us — what, specifically, is NURSE ABUSE all about? —is not about the characteristics that differentiate abused populations or tie them together, but about the forces that conspire to bring about the kind of situation in which intelligent, sensitive, motivated, well-intentioned people find themselves in positions of powerlessness, tolerating indignities and abiding behavior in other people that inevitably diminish them. It is behavior they would never tolerate if it were directed toward their children or their patients.

Nurses occupy jobs prepared for arduously, studied for intently, executed with extraordinary skill and knowledge, and lofty in calling. Then how is it that so many of them experience feelings of self-doubt, intense anger, depression, and self-abnegation? What type of person becomes a nurse? Since 97 percent of nurses are women, is there something inherent in the female gender that predisposes women to abide the abuse of others? If so, is this simply the female condition, the common lot of all women? Is it the inevitable result of an entire history of sexist thought and behavior? Or, is taking abuse endemic to only certain women, and particularly the types of women who become nurses?

Certainly, these questions demand exploration by philosophers, historians, and sociologists. In fact, such explorations have attempted, albeit inadequately, to explain such behavior. But it is the field of psychology, the study of mental processes and behavior that has attempted, most single-mindedly, to explain why people think and act as they do.

Where do the seeds of adult attitudes and behavior begin? For women, it all begins at the moment they are conceived and, many times before conception, in the fantasies of their progenitors. Given the vast differences between females and males, it is understandable that the fantasy of becoming a parent of a daughter is dissimilar for men and women. After all, women have been girls, daughters, sisters, females in a world that remains largely sexist. Men have been boys, sons, brothers, males in a world in which males are still the primary wage earners, the moving forces in industry, the occupiers of political seats of power, the pilots of airplanes. Even in the kitchen, "when a culture develops a tradition of haute cuisine, 'real' cooking, the high chefs are almost always men" (Ortner, 1974, p. 80).

When contemplating the birth of a little girl, the traditional values haven't significantly changed. In the musical "Carousel," Billy Bigelow, in his soliloquy, fantasizes about his as-yet-unborn daughter. His words embody the still-prevailing fantasy of not only affection, but dependency and control. "My little girl, pink and white as peaches and cream is she...My little girl gets hungry every night and she comes home to me" (Rodgers & Hammerstein, 1946).

For women, especially those of the '90s, having a daughter

involves an entirely different fantasy. Many of these women have embarked on careers before even contemplating motherhood. They are aware that more than 50 percent of the American workforce is comprised of females, most of whom still earn $.65 cents or less for every $1.00 earned by their male counterparts. Modern women are keenly aware of discriminatory wage-and-promotion practices in universities, the legal profession, industry, and health care. Many of these women have raised their children in single-parent families, juggled domestic demands and job responsibilities unaided, sat in family courts to collect overdue child-support payments from dead-beat husbands, and borne the anxiety associated with inadequate day-care facilities.

After the birth of a daughter, fantasy ends and "real life" sets in. While arguments within the psychological community abound as to the relative importance of each developmental milestone, there has not been, until recent contributions of feminist writers, psychologists, and philosophers serious controversy about the stages infants and children negotiate on their way to adulthood.

Before the contribution of these theorists, most students of human behavior failed to discuss those experiences most central to female development: affiliation and connectedness. By this omission, they failed to understand and appreciate the unique effect these experiences had on societies both modern and ancient, or to gain insight into the phenomenon of abuse — both giving it and taking it.

Here, we are looking at two current realties. The first is that, at this point in our historical development, men continue to have predominant power and influence in society. The second is that nurses, who work primarily in male-dominated institutions, spend their professional lives working under the men who have that power and influence, be they doctors or administrators.

At the end of the last century and the beginning of this one, Sigmund Freud revolutionized human existence by introducing his unprecedented theories about mental life. Through his explorations and descriptions of the psychoanalytic process, he advanced his theories of the unconscious, those subterranean mental processes that drive human behavior.

Critics have validly pointed out that Freud's frame of reference, and his conclusions, were based on the times and place in which he lived: Vienna in the late 1900s and early 20th Century. These circumstances, critics have explained, account for Freud's sexist slant and patriarchal bias and the degree to which they have been utilized to the detriment of women. Even today, Freudian thought continues to serve as the bedrock of most psychological theory.

To be sure, Freudian theory is completely eschewed by some feminist thinkers, and also by some schools of psychology, such as the cognitive/behaviorist school. But those feminists who continue to recognize Freud's work as an important contribution to psychological understanding have, nevertheless, taken issue with what Nancy Chodorow (1978, p. 142) calls his "unexamined patriarchal assumptions, [his] own blindness, contempt of women, and misogyny...[his] claims about biology, which Freud was in no position to demonstrate from his own research, from a patriarchal value system, and an evolutionary theory to rationalize these values...from his failure to deal with women at all in the major part of his writing, even when it specifically concerns issues of gender."

In fact, many of Freud's followers, such as Karen Horney, Otto Rank, Alfred Adler, Erich Fromm, Melanie Klein, and Carl Jung departed from some of Freud's theories, and interpreted important psychological milestones such as the Oedipus complex and the role of the mother in ways which depart from his doctrine.

However, it is also true that Freud's understanding of the early developmental stages of the human species has succeeded in illuminating the relationship between early experience and adult behavior. The valid criticisms of Freudian theory, particularly its negative effects on the perception and treatment of women, does not negate the fact that Freud's contribution to our understanding of intrapsychic phenomena and behavior was towering in its imagination.

While it is my intention to use Freudian theory as a basis for understanding abuse, the important contributions of other and differing theories will also be included to present as unbiased and non-sexist a view as possible. I have relied heavily on the works of feminist scholars who have succeeded in shedding new light on psychological theory. But first is Freud's.

In Freud's psychoanalytic view, the infant, during its long period of dependency, undergoes many developmental milestones, both physical and psychological, all of which have important implications for its future life. Recognizing that the infant is a complex organism of biological and constitutional ingredients who is influenced by both the environment and the social milieu into which it is born, Freud placed the greatest emphasis on the topography of the psyche, and in trying to understand how the processes he conceived brought about this or that behavior. In so doing, he introduced both revolutionary concepts and an entirely new vocabulary which, before he articulated it, were virtually unknown.

Freud conceived the ego as "the major integrative institution of the personality. Its major function was maintenance of the organism vis-a-vis `three harsh masters' — external reality, the id, and the superego" (Munroe, 1955, p. 86). Functioning in many capacities-sensory, memory, judgment, imagination, etc. — the ego enables the organism to adapt to the "real world," and mediates between this world and the other demands of the psyche. The id is comprised of biologically determined impulses, "...the reservoir of instinctual needs which press toward immediate fulfillment...all the components of sexual instincts...[and the] instinct of aggression" (Munroe, 1955, p. 85). The superego is commonly known as the conscience, the mechanism by which parental and societal dictates become incorporated into the child's psyche.

Central to analytic theory is the idea of the unconscious, the "...mental activity which affects the physical activities and feelings [of people], but is not available to their conscious selves" (Chodorow, 1978, p. 40). Because of some actual or perceived threat, or the experience of pain or frustration which is intolerable to the conscious mind, the subject (be it infant, child, or adult) relegates the unacceptable issue through the defense mechanism of repression. Chodorow (1978, p. 42) says that, "People use unnoticeable operations in their psychological experience of others as defenses, to cope with lack of control, ambivalence, anxiety, loss, feelings of dependence, helplessness, envy." Freud felt repression was the result of anxiety and that anxiety signaled, even to the infant, a potential danger which the ego tries to avoid.

In addition to repression, Freud described an entire repertoire of defense mechanisms, psychological strategies that people employ to deal with their entire gamut of emotions. Among these defense mechanisms are:

1.   Introjection (or internalization). This is when a characteristic of another person is literally taken into the self or part of the self. For instance, the benevolence or harshness of a parent.

2.   Identification. This is when attributes of another person, both those that are admired or feared, are imitated or adopted.

3.   Projection. This is when qualities the individual possesses are externalized onto someone else. For instance, when a person accuses everyone else of being competitive, when it is really he or she who feels competitive.

4.   Reaction formation. This is when a person converts a feeling or idea into the opposite. For instance, a person may insist s/he doesn't care how a boss feels about him or her, when s/he actually cares very much.

5.   Displacement. This is when a strong feeling (such as anger) is expressed toward an inappropriate object or person. For instance, a frustrated person may "kick the dog" instead of expressing anger at the target of his or her rage.

6.   Rationalization. This is when a person "reinterprets" objective facts to fit his or her ego needs. For instance, "I didn't deserve that traffic ticket, I've always been a law-abiding citizen."

7.   Regression. This is when a person reverts to infantile behavior. This is a common response in illness, when people feel helpless, dependent, and needy.

8.   Denial. This is when unacceptable thoughts or feelings are put out of awareness. For instance, "I don't believe it's cancer."

9.   Sublimation. This is when instinctual drives are redirected into other directions. For instance, turning the grief of breast cancer into political action.

The psychoanalytic view places great emphasis on the early years of development, postulating that infantile and early childhood experiences have far-reaching effects that color the person's entire life. While it's impossible to describe and elaborate on the many intricate phases and stages of development which the various schools of psychology have described, the following unelaborated-upon description of the psychological stages of the first years of human development is intended to offer insight into the subject at hand — abuse and particularly how certain processes may lead to the kind of self-image which predispose a person toward either inviting or abiding the abusive behavior of others.

While there have been many alterations in child-caring and child-rearing arrangements over the past century, it still remains true that the mother is the primary nurturer of the human infant. If the mother does not provide the earliest nurturance, the task is assigned to a surrogate, almost without exception another woman.

Central to the infantile experience is dependency, when the infant's most primitive needs are met, or unmet. If the infant's needs for holding, feeding, interacting, are met, s/he develops what Erik Erickson has called "basic trust," a sense that the environment and that people are benevolent and unthreatening. So critical to later development is this stage that it is considered by the psychoanalytic school to be the foundation upon which all subsequent psychological processes are predicated.

Initially, the infant is only aware of its own needs for being held, fed, comforted, etc. The mother is experienced as an extension of the self and as a vehicle for providing those needs. As the infant's needs are either gratified or thwarted, s/he experiences feelings varying from contentment to frustration to discomfort to alarm. Because the infant is totally helpless, the feelings engendered at this time lead to a strong attachment to and dependence on the mother (or mother substitute). If gratification is not forthcoming, the infant experiences anxiety and begins to develop a variety of psychological mechanisms to deal with it.

As the baby gets older, s/he becomes aware that the mother is not an extension of the self, but rather a separate individual. This awareness is fraught with anxiety, since s/he now recognizes that the mother-object may not always be available. By the end of the first year, the baby has learned that people can be benevolent, harsh, loud, consistent, or capricious, and s/he begins to develop adaptive behaviors to deal with his or her world.

As the baby progresses through the oral phase into the anal phase and then the genital phase of development, critical milestones are reached, both physically (for instance, toilet use), and psychologically (for instance, dealing with the advent of a sibling, with maternal separation, etc.). This "pre-Oedipal" period is a time of intense attachment to the mother. Because the father is not involved in the day-to-day care of the child, he is seen as a more remote figure. "As a result, representations of the father relationship do not become so internalized and subject to ambivalence, repression...nor so determining of the person's identify and sense of self" (Chodorow, 1978, p. 94).

At about age three or four, the child must negotiate the Oedipal drama. Up to this point, both female and male children have been cared for almost exclusively by a female, and have come to identify with many of her qualities. Because she has been the person on whom they have depended, she has also inspired their most intense and passionate emotions of rage (at being frustrated), of ambivalence (when both love and hate are evoked), of fear (at the prospect of her withholding or removing her love). And since the very acts of eating, being held, bathed, caressed, even of defecating, have erotic components to them, the mother is also perceived and experienced as an erotic object and is the focus of her child's libidinal desires (although those feelings are not interpreted by the child with adult understanding).

According to Freud, the major task of the Oedipal phase of development is to prepare for heterosexual adult relationships. During this phase, the boy comes to see his father as a rival for his mother's love. He fantasizes doing harm to his father and then feels guilty and imagines that his father will retaliate (castration being a particular fear). If the Oedipal Complex is successfully resolved, the little boy deals with the anxiety his thoughts arouse by eventually abandoning his erotic wishes toward his mother and repressing them.

Finally, "the carrot of the masculine oedipus complex is identification with his father, and the superiority of masculine identification and prerogatives over feminine (if the threat of castration is to stick)" (Chodorow, 1978, p. 94). "A boy, in his attempt to gain an elusive masculine identification, often comes to define his masculinity largely in negative terms, as that which is not feminine or involved with women...Internally, the boy tries to reject his mother and deny his attachment and the strong dependence upon her that he still feels.

He also tries to deny the deep personal identification with her that has developed during his early years. He does this by repressing whatever he takes to be feminine inside himself, and by denigrating and devaluing whatever he considers to be feminine in the outside world" (Chodorow, 1974, p. 50). "To acquire his masculine identity, the boy must both reject and deny, totally and drastically, his former dependencies, attachment, and identification with his mother: A boy represses those qualities he takes to be feminine inside himself, and rejects and devalues women and whatever he considers to be feminine in the social world" (Segal, 1987, p. 138).

For a girl, the Oedipal drama is an entirely different experience. This phase of development is delayed for girls and is thought to be related to the tendency of women to identify more with daughters and so to help them separate and differentiate less. During this time, "the pre-oedipal attachment of daughter to mother continues to be concerned with early mother-infant and relational issues. It sustains the mother-infant exclusivity and the intensity, ambivalence, and boundary confusion of the child still preoccupied with issues of dependence and individuation" (Chodorow, 1978, p. 97).

Inevitably, the little girl must change her love object from mother to father and to become oriented toward men. According to analytic theory, "...the little girl's incestuous attachment to her mother...is repressed only after she comes to realize her own lack of the superior sex organ, the penis, and, along with it, her mother's similar lack of this much-valued possession" (Segal, 1987, p. 138). She turns to her father, acknowledging the superiority of the male and her own inferior status.

In addition, "When an omnipotent mother perpetuates primary love and primary identification...a girl's father is likely to become a symbol of freedom from this dependence and merging"

(Chodorow, 1978, p. 121). During this period in a girl's development a father's role is critical. There are ways "a father can be not there enough, which leads a girl to idealize her father or men, or to endow [men] with immensely sadistic or punitive characteristics, or he can be there too much, requiring her to develop defensive measures against involvement with him and with men" (Chodorow, 1978, p. 118).

It is important to mention here that modern feminists have rightfully taken issue with the concept of penis envy and have redefined it as power envy, a coveting of the prerogatives of authority and influence denied to women as a result of the early developmental phenomena described above. "The penis is a symbol of power or omnipotence...." Its symbol promises "the freedom...from her previous sense of dependence, and not because it is inherently and obviously better to be masculine: women do not wish to become men, but want to detach themselves from the mother and become complete, autonomous women" (Chodorow, 1978, p. 123).

To sum up: "A boy gives up his mother in order to avoid punishment, but identifies with his father because he can then gain the benefits of being the one who gives punishment, of being masculine and superior...a girl identifies with her mother in their common feminine inferiority and in her heterosexual stance...the fact that the child's earliest relationship is with a woman becomes exceedingly important [in] subsequent developmental periods; that women mother and men do not is projected back by the child after gender comes to count. Women's early mothering, then, creates specific conscious and unconscious attitudes or expectations in children. Girls and boys expect and assume women's unique capacities for sacrifice, caring, and mothering, and associate women with their own fears of regression and powerlessness. They fantasize more about men, and associate them with idealized virtues and growth" (Chodorow, 1978, p. 113).

In addition to influential psychological forces during early development, powerful cultural forces are at work. I remember hearing of one experiment in which the vocal tones of both parents and other people were recorded upon first seeing an infant. Consistently, infant girls (dressed in pink) were greeted with soft coos and gibberish while infant boys (dressed in blue) were spoken to in more adult, articulate ways. When the gender of the babies could not be identified because their dress was neutral, people seemed at a loss and actually asked the parent(s) what sex the baby was. The conclusion was that baby girls were considered more "babyish" and "cute," while baby boys inspired responses more in keeping with the adult notion of them as "little men."

What are the implications of such early psychological and cultural conditioning? And how does it lead to women in this case, nurses — who devalue themselves and, by so doing, tolerate the intolerable, accept the unacceptable, and abide the abuses which are their common lot?

In negotiating the Oedipal drama, a girl both separates herself and firmly identifies herself with her mother, and, by association, with all womankind. Unlike the boy, who has had to deny his more feminine characteristics, the girl is able, indeed encouraged, to both retain and enhance them. Now, she will become the nurturing, protective, caretaking person, and those will be qualities which will insure her the love from men that she wants and needs.

The entire course of female development, cultural as well as psychological, as well as the female child's identification with her own mother, predicts the continuation of the "female role," childbearing and caretaking (of both children, mates, and, in the case of nurses, patients). She believes "that any activity is more satisfying when it takes place in the context of relationships to other human beings, and even more so when it leads to the enhancement of others" (Miller, 1976, p. 53).

In contrast, "the question of whether he is a giver or giving enough does not enter into a man's self-image...[men] are concerned much more about 'doing'" (Miller, 1976, p. 49). Moreover, it becomes important for the male identity that certain behaviors and activities are clearly defined as masculine, and therefore, superior. A corollary to this belief is that women, because of their intrinsic "inferiority," are unable to participate in the "really important" tasks of society and that their contributions can, in no way, equal those of the males.

For women, "identity is defined in a context of relationships...while for men, identity precedes intimacy and generativity in the optimal cycle of human separation and attachment...for women these tasks seem instead to be fused. Intimacy goes along with identity, as the female comes to know herself through her relationships with others" (Gilligan, 1982, p. 160). By example, the little girl learns to value most highly the affiliative aspects of her life and to subordinate her own wishes to those she perceives as having power.

"Women's lives are bereft because they are the needy little girls of mothers who, inevitably, taught them to put their own needs second...daughters unmet needs provide the well from which they give to others" (Segal, 1987, p. 139). "Since women have had to live by trying to please men, they have been conditioned to prevent men from feeling even uncomfortable...when women suspect that they have caused men to feel unhappy or angry, they have a strong tendency to assume that they themselves are wrong" (Miller, 1976, p. 57).

The female is considered closer to nature than the male who is more closely identified with the larger culture. In addition, the roles that the female takes on as a result of her mothering (cooking, cleaning, caring for the children, etc.) are considered of a lower order on the cultural scale. In explaining female subordination, Sherry B. Ortner (1974, p. 73) states that "Since it is always culture's project to subsume and transcend nature, if women were considered part of nature, then culture would find it 'natural' to subordinate them." With irony and undisguised facetiousness, Ortner (1974, p. 73) states that the male, "...lacking natural creative functions, must (or has the opportunity to) assert his creativity externally, 'artificially,' through the medium of technology and symbols. In so doing, he creates relatively lasting, eternal, transcendent objects, while the women creates only perishables human beings. Hence, the cultural reasoning seems to go [that] men are the 'natural' proprietors of religion, ritual, politics, and other realms of cultural thought and action...."

Chodorow (1978, p. 185) explains the pervasive devaluation of women by referring to early experiences of both boys and girls: "Too much mother results from the relative absence of the father and nearly exclusive maternal care provided by a woman isolated in a nuclear household. It creates men's resentment and dread of women, and their search for non-threatening, undemanding, dependent, even infantile women, women who are 'simple, and thus safe and warm.'

Through these same processes, men come to reject, devalue, and even ridicule women and things feminine. Women's mothering produces a psychological and ideological complex in men concerning women's secondary valuation and sexual inequality. Because women are responsible for early child care and for most later socialization as well, because fathers are more absent from the home, and because men's activities generally have been removed from the home while women's have remained within it, boys have difficulty in attaining a stable masculine gender role identification.

"Boys fantasize about and idealize the masculine role and their fathers, and society defines it as desirable. Given that men control not only major social institutions, but the very definition and constitution of society and culture, they have the power and ideological means to enforce these perceptions as more general norms, and to hold each other accountable for their enforcement." Of course, the inevitable result of emotional subordination "occurs when subordinates incorporate the dominant group's conception of themselves as inferior or secondary. Such women are less able to recognize and clarify their own needs...instead, they believe the man will somehow fulfill these needs and then are disappointed, often miserably" (Miller, 1976, p. 15).

It is because the affiliative aspect of their identities have been undervalued that women come to undervalue themselves. Women who have wanted to enter "the mainstream" of society have believed they had to imitate masculine qualities in order to be accepted. This is particularly relevant to the nurse whose very "role" in her clinical capacity embodies some of the nurturing, affiliative, feminine aspects which have been historically so devalued.

One of the major contributions of the modern feminist movement has been to introduce the notion that women must now learn to value those qualities, to redefine both themselves and society in terms of these "strengths," and to strive, both in their personal and professional lives, to settle for nothing less than relationships and work situations which accept this redefinition. One of the great powers of nursing is its intrinsic ability to bring humane and caring qualities to an increasingly dehumanized and unfeeling 'system' of medical care. Learning how to acquire power while retaining these qualities is one of nursing's greatest challenges.

It does not require higher reasoning to conclude that little girls, indeed infant girls, are socialized and conditioned to have a devalued image of themselves even when the development proceeds "normally." By the same token, it does not take a quantum leap of logic to deduce that a devalued self-image is the corollary of low self-esteem. It is this low self-esteem which leads to the susceptibility for abuse — for putting up with (and perhaps unconsciously inviting) behavior in others which serves to perpetuate that devaluation.

It is difficult to envision how early influences of the relatively normal variety have the power to affect adult behavior. As our cognitive processes develop, and we progress through different stages of mastery over our environment, we come to rely on our intellects, our judgements, in order to effect decisions, make changes, and find solutions. When we find ourselves in problem relationships (personal or professional), many of them eerily similar to ones that have gone before, we tend to ignore the similarities. In evaluating these situations, we tend to ignore, not only the kinds of psychological processes which have brought them about, but also the powerful cultural influences which have helped to shape and reinforce them. It is no accident that many people repeat the same mistake or that the indignities they tolerate in one sphere (for instance, a personal relationship), they find themselves tolerating in another sphere (for instance, the job).

The "repetition compulsion" is the tendency of some people to repeat early, painful experiences. This is thought to be an unconscious need to resolve, through reenactment, the earlier trauma. This can be clearly seen in the woman who chooses a man who abuses her, divorces him, and finds a similar type the next time around. There have been many theories about the "self-defeating" or "masochistic" personality, beginning with Freud's pronouncement that "Anatomy is destiny"! In his view, masochism was a key part of female destiny.

Gerda Lerner (1986, p. 52), however, has called this statement "...wrong, because it is...ahistorical and reads the distant past into the present without making allowances for changes over time. Worse, this statement has been read as a prescription for present and future: not only is anatomy destiny for women, but it *should* be. What Freud should have said is that the woman's anatomy once was destiny. That statement is accurate and historical. What once was no longer is so, and no longer must be nor should it be so."

Karen Horney, too, disagreed with Freud, emphasizing the role that cultural conditioning played in the female's self-defeating experiences. Society views women as weak and helpless. It encourages them to be emotionally and economically dependent; it restricts their functioning. A personality influenced by these factors will most likely suffer from low self-esteem and feelings of powerlessness, and such a personality may tend to provoke further punishment and suffering (Shainess, 1984, p. 19).

The subject of female masochism has been challenged by feminists and clinicians who have pointed to the degree to which such so-called self-punishing behavior is not desired, but more often a function of cultural and psychological conditioning. "The ability to delay gratification and wait for rewards through effort, the capacity to put other people's needs ahead of one's own, the belief that one should have limited expectations, and the effort to avoid punishment, rejection or guilt...the same behaviors that are defined as masochistic in women would be defined quite healthily as sacrificial or courageous or facing reality or hard work in men" (Collins, 1985).

Irving Bieber, a contemporary psychoanalyst, places problems of power at the center of self-defeating behavior. A child's first acquaintance with power occurs in the family, and it's there a child, who is initially weak and helpless, develops the fear of power of others. Bieber says the things which make the child fear authority are the trigger in any self-defeating exchange and views this behavior as a defense mechanism that seeks to prevent or extinguish hostile aggression in others; its operating principle is that self-inflicted harm can ward off even more dangerous threats (Shainess, 1984, p. 19).

In her book, *Sweet Suffering*, Natalie Shainess (1984, p. 41) explains that the masochistic* person.

Shainess says that the self-defeating person is "...confronted [in infancy or childhood] with a powerful other, and often experiences a state of...hypno-suggestibility which causes her/him to accept whatever the other person says as correct" (Shainess, 1984, p. 41). This phenomenon begins in childhood vis-a-vis significant adults and it is there that the self-defeating person begins to accept the premise of the other as a defensive maneuver (Shainess, 1984, p. 47).

Shainess speaks of "signals" which self-defeating people send out to the world at large:

1. Capitulation, "the tendency to collapse in the face of opposition."
2. Accommodation, "willing to let other people call the tune."
3. "Letting others off the hook and underscoring their own mistakes."
4. "Rushing to hand other people excuses to justify their attacks on her and to rationalize away her own feelings in deference to theirs."
5. Excessive apology.
6. Avoidance of questioning.

Shainess (1984, p. 54) explains that anxiety is based on experiences in childhood with significant adults, "...figures who are

(I have chosen to use the term "self-defeating" rather than "masochistic" because the latter has been associated with the notion that such behavior grows out of the unconscious desire for suffering, a theory which has been rightfully challenged and appropriately dismissed over the past few years by leading theorists.]
now phantoms that insinuate themselves into people we encounter in our adult lives. [Self-defeating people] constantly respond to the

present as if it were happening in the past, participating in a kind of shadow play in which people are not who they seem to be.

"Such women are less able to recognize and clarify their own needs, either to themselves or to men. Sometimes truly blaming the person(s) who hurt you can seem so much harder than continuing the [self-defeating] circle of self-condemnation...[she] may seem to blame the oppressor, but she blames herself even more...." (Shainess, 1984, p. 57).

In speaking about the hidden cruelty in child-rearing, Alice Miller (1983, p. 98) says that "...all advice that pertains to raising children betrays...the numerous, variously clothed needs of the adult. Fulfillment of those needs not only discourages the child's development, but actually prevents it...[even]...when the adult is honestly convinced of acting in the child's best interests.

Among the adult's true motives," she mentions: "The unconscious need to pass onto others the humiliation [they] have undergone themselves; the need to find an outlet for repressed [feelings]; and the need to possess and have at one's own disposal of vital subject to manipulate; the need to idolize one's childhood and one's parents by dogmatically applying the parents' pedagogical principles to one's own children; the fear of freedom; the fear of the reappearance of what one has repressed, which one reencounters in one's child and must try to stamp out, having killed it in oneself earlier; and revenge for the pain one has suffered. Thus, when children are trained, they learn how to train others in turn.

"Children who are lectured learn how to lecture; if they are ridiculed, they learn how to ridicule; if humiliated, they learn how to humiliate, if their psyche is killed, they will learn how to kill — the only question is who will be killed: oneself, others, or both." Although Miller does not specifically use the word "abuse," it is clear that she is speaking about abusive behavior and making the point that if one is abused, or demeaned or devalued, or if she identifies herself strongly with a mother who has been abused, she may carry within her into adulthood, not only the rage that abuse inspires, but also the tendency to experience its repetition. This repetition may take two forms; either taking abuse or giving it, depending on how the experience has been processed psychologically.

While it is true that males also experience both psychological and physical abuse in our society, that word is more closely associated with females. And for good reason. "Women abuse...is the most common and least reported crime in the United States" (Brown, 1987, p. 7). According to Angela Browne, "In this country, a woman's chances of being assaulted at home by her partner are greater than that of a police officer being assaulted on the job." Gloria Steinem (1983, p. 159) has said that "Battered women is a phrase that uncovered major, long-hidden violence. It helps us to face that, statistically speaking, the most dangerous place for a woman is in her own home, not in the streets."

Sexual abuse, too, is primarily a case of female victimization, both in childhood and adulthood. Some theorists have postulated that women who are battered as adults came from homes in which they were sexually abused and so lacked "the normal adult mechanisms of self-protection". When it happens to them again, they see "their lack of experience with prior abuse as a major factor in their inability to comprehend and deal with the violence when it occurs" (Brown, 1987, p. 30). The violent act of rape involves nearly 100 percent of women-as-victims. While the myth that women who are raped "brought it upon themselves" is gradually disappearing, it still remains true that rape is "a constant reminder of the extent to which women are devalued, objectified, and deprived of personal autonomy."

In both medical and mental-health arenas, women have encountered abuses simply as a function of being female. "Women who fully act out the conditioned female role are clinically viewed as neurotic...[those] who reject or are ambivalent about the female role...are also assured of a psychiatric label..." (Chesler, 1972, p. 56). In 1987, the American Psychiatric Association, contemplated a revision of *The Diagnostic and Statistical Manual of Mental Health Disorders - III* (DSM-III) by proposing a new category called Paraphilic Rapism which was described as "a persistent association, lasting a total of six months, between intense sexual arousal or desire, and acts, fantasies, or other stimuli involving coercing or forcing a non-consenting person to engage in vaginal, anal, or oral intercourse."

If this category had been included — which it was not because of intense lobbying efforts by a committee of the Association of Women Psychiatrists (AWP), feminist groups, and other womens' organizations — it would have completely removed the criminality of rape and the violence, aggression, and rage toward women which underlie its act. That it was ever considered is a testimony to the continued contempt which many male psychiatrists hold toward women.

What was included in the revised edition were two new categories which label women in retrogressive, sexist, inaccurate, and downright destructive ways. The first was called Self-Defeating Personality Disorder. According to the AWP, the criteria for this category described personality and behavior patterns which, for women, were culturally assigned. There was no similar diagnosis for what they described as "the aggressive, power-driven, exploiting personality and behavior patterns fostered by the culture in men."

The second new category was called the Late Luteal Phase Dysphoric Disorder, which alludes to premenstrual symptoms and mistakenly describes a physiological phenomenon in psychological terms. While it is true that the premenstrual condition may give rise to the symptoms described by the APA (emotional lability, fatigue, tension, etc.) in the same way that other physical conditions have psychological counterparts, it is also true that the biological solution to this condition leaves the female therapy patient with a label which militates against all sorts of possibilities for the rest of her productive life. It forces the woman so diagnosed to defend herself against this diagnosis for years after the problems of premenstrual dysphoria have been diminished or eliminated.

It is certainly understandable that a woman who seeks psychological counseling and is already low on the self-esteem scale would hesitate to question an "authority figure" who pronounces her self-defeating; both women and men in such situations do not feel confident in their judgment. However, any woman who appreciates the vast implications which these kinds of diagnoses can have on both her current life and on her future would be well-advised to ask her therapist exactly what her diagnosis is, and to protest these particular categories if they are inaccurately applied to her. Failing to effect any change, she should find another therapist.

In his book *MALePRACTICE* (1981), the late Robert S. Mendelsohn, M.D., stated that, "...although medical and surgical overkill are routinely inflicted on all Americans, its primary victims are women...Female patients are subjected to medical procedures that are degrading, unnecessary, and often dangerous, sometimes fatally so." Asserting that "most doctors are unaware of their negative feelings toward female patients...[their] sexist behavior [is] at the heart of the medical abuse women suffer" (Mendelsohn, 1981, p. 61).

The "double standard" in medicine is well-known to most women. "It is not uncommon for a doctor to advise a male patient to 'work out' his problems in the gym or on the golf course, while a female patient with the same symptoms is likely to be given a prescription for Valium" (Mendelsohn, 1981, p. 61).

The abuse of women (and of the girls who will become women) is not restricted to the home or to the area of psychological or medical services. Perhaps the greatest form of institutionalized abuse belongs to the workplace and is, in fact, the prime motivator behind NURSE ABUSE. As a former obstetrical nurse, I was constantly astounded and appalled at the misogyny which I both experienced and observed in the clinical setting. It is interesting to note that the word itself, misogyny (which is derived from the Greek), means literally: miso: to hate, and gyne (as in gynecologist): woman.

According to economist Sylvia Ann Hewlett (1986, p. 83), "Gender seems to be a more powerful handicap than race in the labor market. Despite the enormous expansion of the female labor force in recent years, the number of women working has [more than] doubled since 1960, there has been little improvement in women's economic position...only seven percent of employed women in America work in managerial positions." It is a commentary on the pervasive devaluation of women and of the importance they play in the nation's economy that, although three-quarters of the nation's working women have school-age children and half have children less than a year old, it wasn't until 1993 before the United States adopted a statutory maternity leave.

In the vital area of day care, problems of inadequate legislation, of meager funding, of poor regulation, of underpaid staff workers abound. According to the Labor Department, only 11 percent of United States companies provide some child-care services to their employees, but only two percent actually sponsor day-care centers and only three percent provide financial assistance for child care. In a May 1988 Census Bureau report, it was reported that the inability to find a babysitter disrupted the jobs of about 450,000 women nationally each month.

While available day-care services have increased in the '90s, so have their costs. This often translates to total exploitation of the single woman who must literally decide between working and handing over her entire paycheck for child care, or remaining in the home and taking government handouts. Society has discovered yet another economic way to keep women in their "place," dependent on a paternalistic system of support.

On the job, the catalogue of inequities for women is filled with topics such as: wages consistently lower than their male counterparts earn; discrimination in promotional policies; horizontal, not upward, mobility; and the difficulty, again, in dealing with those in power, most of whom are men.

In 1988, the term "sexual harassment" became synonymous with women. It is interesting that among the synonyms used by *Webster's Dictionary* to describe harassment are badger, pester, plague, and torment. Certainly, they can all be subsumed under the category of abuse. The woman who is sexually harassed is on the receiving end of leering, pinching, patting, repeated comments, subtle suggestions of a sexual nature and pressure for dates.

Abuse can also take the form of actual or attempted rape. "Women who are sexually harassed find themselves in the classic double-bind: if they capitulate, they are filled with self-contempt; if they resist, they find themselves the victims of work-related reprisals. These can include: escalation of harassment; poor work assignments; sabotaging of projects; denial of raises, benefits or promotions; and sometimes the loss of the job, with only a poor reference to show for it" (*The New Our Bodies/Ourselves*, 1984, p. 108).

Both job-related and sexual harassment are well-known to nurses. The doctors — be they interns, residents, or attending physicians — who perpetrate abuses are elaborating on behavior that characterizes the nurse/doctor relationship in general. As a microcosm of society-at-large, this relationship perpetuates the roles of male as dominant, female as subordinate. For those who protest that "times have changed," it would be instructive to review the fierce opposition doctors have waged against nurses who have sought legislation to expand the nursing role or to create alternatives to health-maintenance organizations (HMOs) in community nursing organizations (CNO's).

At a July, 1988 convention of the American Medical Association, doctors, reacting to the "nursing crisis," proposed a "new class of worker" called registered care technicians (RCTs). "The AMA acknowledged that one goal of creating RCTs was to draw in more male workers who otherwise wouldn't be attracted to nursing" (Dentzer, 1988). Although the original concept of the RCT failed, this same practice of replacing R.N.s with unlicensed assistive personnel (UAP) has been revived and is being perpetrated in the '90s by nursing administrations throughout the country. Now, however, this blatant form of NURSE ABUSE has been given the colorful, and inaccurate, name of Patient-Focused Care.

With few avenues to redress their grievances, the anger that nurses feel is negotiated through the defense mechanisms learned at an earlier stage of development. The nurse may use "displacement" to target her rage onto a fellow nurse. Angry at herself for capitulating to unreasonable demands, she may use "projection" to express the contempt she feels toward herself onto an innocent patient. She may "identify" with her oppressor and find herself oppressing others. She may "rationalize" her failure to take action by convincing herself that passivity is apt to be the better route to gaining her goals. Or, she may become appropriately angry and suffer the consequences! Among the many psychologically-battering consequences that are foisted on women (and, of course, nurses) are: "Assuming the right to control women's behavior; devaluing her opinions, feelings and accomplishments; yelling, threatening, withdrawing into angry silence when displeased; making the woman afraid of 'setting him off;' switching from charm to rage without warning; making her feel inadequate or confused (Forward, 1986, p. 132).

Although nurses are grown women, they have been socialized and conditioned to engage in "learned helplessness." They learn that "you are good to the degree that you give men what they want and follow the rules that they have laid down for you. You sacrifice your own personal satisfaction in return for being told how nice and sweet you are by the men whose approval you are seeking...this is no substitute for meeting your own needs. The inevitable consequence is a continual low-level anger that flares up periodically in unexplainable outbursts..." (Fezler, 1985, p. xii).

"For most women, there is an enormous gap between their childhood conditioning and the process necessary to achieve growth and personal fulfillment...tremendous conflict between the conscious needs [of the '90s] and the subconscious messages received in early childhood..." (Dworkin, 1974, p. 23).

The nature of abuse, both giving it and taking it, can be found in the seeds of our very earliest development, first in the fantasies of those who, before we are born, imagine what we will be like, and then in the realities of our individual life experiences. That the female experience is vastly different than the male's, and that those differences affect every subsequent aspect of our lives is indisputable.

That nurses, occupying, as they do, a profession historically associated with female exclusivity, have been subject to abuse, is no mystery. That the "caretaker" function of nurses evokes so keenly the ambivalent or negative reactions of many of their co-workers, both male and female, can only be understood by viewing this reenactment of ancient and highly-charged relationships in their proper psychological context.

Without alluding to gender, Nicolo Machiavelli, in his book *The Prince* (which he wrote in 1513!), captures the primary emotional operating principles which prevail, even now, in the personal and professional lives of women and men in the 1990s. "The question [arises] whether it is better to be loved rather than feared, or feared rather than loved. It might perhaps be answered that we should wish to be both; but since love and fear can hardly exist together, if we must choose between them, it is far safer to be feared than loved."

Must women — must nurses — continue to fear both their own potential for power and the obstacles which confront them? Must they continue to be abused? I think not. But that is fodder for another discussion. Let us call it "Solutions."

References

Blumstein, P. and Schwartz, P. (1983). *American Couples: Money, Work and Sex.* New York: William Morrow.

Boston Women's Health Book Collective. (1984). *The New Our Bodies, Ourselves.* New York: Simon & Schuster.

Brown, A. (1987). *When Battered Women Kill.* New York: Free Press/MacMillan.

Chesler, P. (1972). *Women and Madness.* New York: Avon Books.

Chodorow, N., (Rosaldo, M., & Lamphere, L. (eds). (1974). *Family Structure and Feminine Personality in Women Culture and Society.* Stanford: Stanford University Press.

Chodorow, N. (1978). *The Reproduction of Mothering: Psychoanalysis and the Sociology of Gender.* California: University of California Press.

Collins, G. (1985). Women & Masochism: Debate Continues. An Interview with Dr. Paula Caplan. *New York Times,* December 12.

Dentzer, S. (1988). Calling The Shots in Health Care: The Nursing Shortage Points Up A Growing Turf War Between Doctors and Nurses. *U.S. News and World Report,* July 11.

Dworkin, A. (1974). *Woman Hating.* New York: E.P. Dutton.

Fezler, W., & Field, E. (1985). *The Good Girl Syndrome.* New York: MacMillan.

Forward, S. & Torres, J. (1986). *Men Who Hate Women and the Women Who Love Them.* New York: Bantam Books.

Gilligan, C. (1982). *In A Different Voice: Psychological Theory and Women's Development.* Cambridge: Harvard University Press.

Hewlett, S. A. (1986). *A Lesser Life: The Myth of Women's Liberation in America.* New York: Warner Books.

Lerner, G. (1986). *The Creation of Patriarchy*. New York: Oxford University Press.

Machiavelli, N. (1952). *The Prince*. New York: New American Library.

Mendelsohn, R. S. (1981). *MALePRACTICE: How Doctors Manipulate Women*. Chicago: Contemporary Books.

Miller, A. (1983). *Hidden Cruelty in Child-Rearing and the Roots of Violence*. New York: Farrar, Straus, Giroux.

Miller, J. B. (1976). *Toward a New Psychology of Women*. Boston:Beacon Press.

Ortner, S. B. (Rosaldo, M. & Lamphere, L. eds). (1974). Is Female to Male as Nature is to Culture? *Woman, Culture and Society*. Stanford: Stanford University Press.

Rodgers, R. & Hammerstein, O. (1946). "Carousel." Copyright: Chappell Music Publishing Company.

Segal, L. (1987). *Is the Future Female: Troubled Thoughts on Contemporary Feminism*. New York: Peter Bedrick Press.

Shainess, N. (1984). *Sweet Suffering*. Indianapolis/New York:Bobbs-Merrill Company, Incorporated.

Slattalla, M. (1988). Help for Addicted M.D.s Called Lax. *Newsday*. Long Island, New York, March 6.

Steinem, G. (1983). *Outrageous Acts and Everyday Rebellions*. New York: Holt, Rhinehart & Winston.

Chapter Seven

SOLUTIONS

by Joan Swirsky, R.N., M.S., CS

"If it ain't broke, don't fix it!" is a catchy phrase designed for those things — be they relationships, careers, ideas, machinery or gadgets — which, clearly, function well and don't need to be tampered with. Unfortunately, it is not applicable to the state of the nursing profession which now, a blink away from the 21st Century, is as "broke" as it has been in its entire history.

From its inception, nursing education has been inadequate to prepare nurses for the rigors of the workplace setting. In that setting, primarily the hospital, but also the home, registered nurses have found conditions which militate against their best efforts to deliver the kind of consistent, high-quality care they envisioned when they responded to what most R.N.s consider a lofty calling: the opportunity to care for the sick, tend to the infirm, heal the wounded, and impart both empathy and knowledge to a population sorely in need of both compassionate and informed care.

Even those nurses who enter the profession for pragmatic reasons, i.e., job security, the ability to juggle domestic tasks with a part-time career, decent benefits, etc., are a rarefied species, for they know that these so-called advantages will be earned caring for people who, through accident or illness, have been deprived of their normally productive capacities, if not permanently, at least temporarily.

Nurses know they will be present at critical times: when there is pain, blood, trauma, anguish, fear and doubt, anxiety and depression, birth and death. And, they know their presence will not be passive, that it will depend upon the highest level of knowledge, of skill, of judgment, of intuition, and of alertness.

Yet, in spite of both the academic and clinical preparation they have had, in spite of the years of seniority they might have accumulated, in spite of their involvement in professional organizations, in spite of the additional degrees they may have earned, in spite of the ways in which their own interventions or diagnoses may have saved a person's life, and in spite of their most impassioned efforts to change "the system," nurses find themselves entrapped, sometimes literally, in a job situation in which NURSE ABUSE abounds, in which they are devalued, patronized, harassed, and, as an extra "bonus," underpaid.

As if all this were not bad enough, nurses of the 1990s have found their situations getting worse. The need for higher wages, intolerance of poor staffing, thwarted efforts in organizing, and now massive layoffs to increase profit shares — all have brought about disaffection of the nation's nursing population and a drastic reduction in the numbers of registered nurses in our nation's hospitals. In response, hospital administrations have responded by revealing, for all the world to see, the depth of their contempt for the nurses who, before they were "downsized" and replaced, had been the very lifeblood of the institutions in which they worked.

Recruiting nurses from other countries, doubling or tripling the workloads of those who remain on staff, imposing mandatory overtime, floating R.N.s to areas outside their expertise, are a few of the strategies hospital administrators have employed to demonstrate how dispensable registered nurses are to their institutions. A decade ago, such strategies proved so ineffective that hospitals actually started to increase nurses' salaries and advertise benefits such as tuition reimbursement or affordable housing facilities. Today, these "carrots" are reserved for unlicensed personnel, while R.N.s are standing in unemployment lines!

Similarly, when the nursing crisis of the '80s reared its head, the persistent and insidious sexism which has characterized nurse-doctor relationships throughout history, manifested itself when doctors went one step further than hospital administrations and proposed a "new class of workers" to the health-care system, Registered Care Technicians (Dentzer, 1988). But when that effort failed — the result of a rare coming-together of nurses — it was quickly replaced by a move to create "generic healthcare workers." Thus, the strategy of nurse replacement continues, with minimally trained personnel (even janitors!) performing the functions of a nurse.

In response to the nursing crisis of the '80s, many nursing schools closed and others cut back drastically on both their teaching staffs and curriculum. In response to the nursing crisis of the '90s, the Pew Commission has demanded that 10-20 percent of nursing schools be closed. The days of recruiting potential nurses, of informing high school seniors of the benefits to themselves and society a nursing career offered, are gone. "Cheaper is better" and "less is more" are corporate health-care's new mantras.

Today, the nurse who has been abandoned by her employer is turning increasing to other avenues in the job market, or becoming an entrepreneur. Finding that his or her intelligence, clinical and organizational skills, capacity for hard work, incisive judgment, ability to relate to others, and indefatigable energy are no longer valued, s/he is now entering law school, business, or academia. When s/he goes to the bank, it is IRAs and CDs that are contemplated, not overdrafts.

Many nurses are moving on, some by choice, others by default, to what they perceive as emotional, economic, and professional greener pastures. Whether pressured out or laid off, they have opted to preserve (or, more accurately, recover) their self-esteem, and pursue a better living in an environment where they can flex their intellectual muscles and decision-making capacities.

But, what of the nurse who remains in nursing? In the world of the future, will s/he, like the dinosaur, be recalled as an extinct species. its function hardly remembered and no longer relevant? Are there solutions to the problems that currently beset nursing? Are there ways to end NURSE ABUSE? The answer is a resounding yes! And they are many. Here are the problems and the solutions.

Problem #1: Academia

Nowhere has the current crisis in nursing been more palpable than in those areas of the country in which hospitals are creating dangerously low nurse-patient ratios. Nurses, who with greater and greater frequency are "burning out," are leaving such poor working conditions or leaving the profession altogether. In the '80s, many nurses left nursing because of poor staffing conditions. Today, they are being kicked out to lower costs.

The dramatic decline in hospital nursing staffs is the result of a national trend to reduce staffs and increase corporate profits. In the health system, this reduction appears under the guise of "managed care," a deceptively benign catch-phrase that *seems* to be good for everyone, patients, nurses (who have always "managed" care), and the corporation.

In fact, if nurses had been at all involved with the "business" of hospitals — as they should have been — they would now be reaping the benefits of change instead of being victimized by it. Why haven't nurses been "at the table"? Because nursing schools have failed to address themselves to the crucial issues that affect the very *modus operandi* of the nursing profession. Although nurses, for the most part, work in institutional settings, the schools that prepare them for their jobs consistently fail to include in their curricula the tools essential to cope with or, better, participate in corporate decisions.

Nursing education, unlike the ancient studies of art or science or the humanities, is a relatively new addition to the formal education process. Its history, based on the fact that, up until the recent past, nursing has always been a "female profession," has had a rather unique evolution. That uniqueness is a function of the many issues which have been historically problematical to women, issues such as economic worth, sexism, and power, to name but a few.

It must be remembered that, initially, the founders of modern nursing Florence Nightingale, Dorothea Dix, Louisa Schuyler — were "refugees from the enforced leisure of Victorian ladyhood...to them, nursing training emphasized character, not skills. The finished product, the Nightingale nurse, was simply the ideal lady, transplanted from home to hospital. To the doctor, she brought the wifely virtue of absolute obedience. To the patient, she brought the selfless devotion of a mother...." (Ehrenreich, 1973, p. 36). The model of the Nightingale nurse persisted well into the beginning of the 20th Century, insuring that nurses were underpaid and "educated" according to the needs of doctors, hospitals, and patients not themselves.

And yet, nursing remained attractive to women and, with time, some key changes did occur in the academic preparation of women. In 1940 and throughout that decade, after an unprecedented number of nurses were mobilized for World War II, nursing curricula underwent a major change. Formerly dominated by a focus on biologic systems, the curriculum then introduced the study of psychosocial issues. Soon after, as a natural result of these models, emphasis on the interpersonal process emerged.

During the 1950s, nursing education embraced the "holistic" concept "in which the patient emerged as a logical focal point of the content presented in nursing schools" (Riehl, 1980, p. 10). While the philosophical and functional applications of this change are still being tested by nurses, it was a concept which inspired at least some nurses to deduce that if the individual is important and if I, too, am an individual, then I am important as well.

In the 1960s, several novel nursing approaches were introduced into the nurse's education: a redefinition of the nurse's role, the notion that a nurse was defined by her function, and a patient-oriented concept based upon human needs. However, in spite of these changes, society-at-large was still keeping the nurse in her traditionally devalued place. As late as 1969, 75 percent of community hospitals paid nurses less than $7,500 per year.

During the 1970s, the two-family income had become a common phenomenon, fueled by the woman's movement and its emphasis on female autonomy, by spiraling inflation, by rising expectations, and by increased consumerism. Yet, in 1970, a study of nursing and nursing education concluded that poor working conditions and low status and pay contributed to the nurse's lack of commitment.

By 1977, four million of America's health workers were women. While doctors, 92 percent of whom were male, were the very highest-paid workers in America (in the health-care system), nurses were among the lowest paid. Notwithstanding these demoralizing conditions, nursing education continued to make adaptations which demonstrated a clear commitment to the better-educated nurse. Nursing schools began teaching their students Martha Rogers' model of man/environment/energy interactions, Peplau's model of personality development and interpersonal relations, Hodgman's model of preventive intervention, and Neuman's model which identified leadership, research, systems, teaching, nursing, communication, health continuum, and life cycle in its conceptual framework (Riehl, 1980, p. 11).

Since the mid-'70s, there has been an increase in nurses seeking doctoral degrees, partly to meet the demands of the institutions in which they teach or administrate, and partly to fulfill personal goals. In 1966, there were only three doctoral programs of nursing in the United States. In 1985, there were 35. And yet, the American Nurses Association showed only 0.15 percent of the 1.7 million registered nurses in the U.S. at the time had doctorates, and fewer than 21 percent of these were in nursing!

In addition, in 1980, of the 2,500 nurses with doctoral degrees, both in nursing and in other disciplines, only seven percent reported research as a major activity (Institute of Medicine, 1983) and so the federal government discontinued its financial support of the doctoral nurse-science programs. Many nurses who have obtained doctorates report that they are not perceived as true colleagues or as experts in their working experience. Today, the obstacles of economic inequity and sexism (both overt and covert) continue to plague nursing.

Clearly, nursing education has striven for change. But, to my mind, it has not focused upon its most important element — the nurse — or on the environments in which that nurse practices his or her art and skills, the hospital or home setting. Nursing educators have consistently demonstrated their inability to effect what scientist/philosopher Thomas S. Kuhn has called a "paradigm shift." If they had done so, their educational policies would have reflected a genuine appreciation of the dire need for nursing students to learn how to swim, not sink, in the bureaucratic setting.

It is true that early nursing was not, could not possibly have been, able to predict the global changes in society, economics, feminist thought, technology, law, and ethics that have transpired over the past century. But modern educators, who have lived those changes, inevitably interpret suggestions for change as a repudiation of all that has gone before. Is Kuhn correct when he states that such people have "...lifelong resistance, particularly those whose productive careers have committed them to an older tradition...."? (Kuhn, 1970, p.

151). In nursing, the answer seems obvious.

It is certainly not too late in the evolution of nursing to include those subjects which have been glaringly — and to the detriment of nurses everywhere — absent from modern nursing curricula. For instance: Where are the courses in feminism which give nurses a historical perspective about the social, psychological, and economic ways that sexism has affected female behavior in the professional sphere? Since 97 percent of nurses are female, this omission is glaring.

Contrary to popular opinion, people who go into nursing are keenly aware of the many significant differences between nursing and medicine, and have consciously chosen to pursue the one and not the other. Nursing has always been characterized as a "woman's job" and those who have chosen this path exult in that description. To most nurses, that description defines a heightened capacity to be empathic, to be nurturing, to be understanding, to give, to care, to tend, and to make critical judgments based on a comprehensive perception of the whole person. Yet, nowhere to be found, especially on the Bachelor's level, are courses about the uniqueness of women's past and current history and the sexist traps which the modern workplace presents.

Non-existent, as well, are business courses that teach the inner workings of bureaucracy and how to navigate its hazards. With the exception of a briefly-introduced schematic, detailing administrative hierarchy (on which, not-so-incidentally, few, if any females, appear), there is no classroom discussion that introduces nurses to the notion that it is *they* who might aspire to true administrative power. In true Machiavellian form, hospital administrators have perfected the "art" of giving some nurses the illusion of power by advancing their status, endowing them with new titles, and thus making them a "member" of the administration. Of course, this insures that they will never again be true advocates for nurses or nursing concerns.

By their failure to alert nurses to this ploy and to teach them to fight against it, nursing schools cast themselves as abettors to this travesty.

Absent, as well, are courses in finance and economics, both of which would prepare nurse administrators to control their own budgets, and staff nurses to bargain with authority for wage-and-price benefits. Never raised in the classroom is the issue of public-relations or the concepts of advertising and marketing which would inspire nurses to be their own best image-makers.

Most disturbing is the fact that nurses are never taught that when they enter a hospital as an employee, they are entering a "business" environment; that hospitals are in the "business" of making money; and that they run with the same or similar structures to most other "businesses." Yes, they are in the business of caring for people, but nursing instructors never tell their students that hospital businesses are *not* operated by people who are particularly benevolent or philanthropic and who will treat them with the respect they are due. In fact, hospitals are operated by businessmen — whose prime motives are those which concern all businessmen — economic profits and a shining public image.

Nowhere to be found in modern nursing schools is the law course that teaches nurses about their basic rights or how to redress grievances through legal channels. Much of the intimidation nurses suffer is a result of their ignorance about the law, and how it pertains to their work (or life) situations. Currently, there are a good number of nurses who have become lawyers and who now represent other nurses to resolve their grievances. Are nursing students taught of their existence? Told how to reach them, should the need arise? Certainly not.

It must also be remembered that nurses deal daily with the gravest medico-legal issues of our day. The care of AIDS patients, assisted suicide, abortion, organ transplants, life-support systems, informed consent, patients' rights, the conflict (in some cases) between medicine and religion — all these issues, and the myriad of questions and conflicts that they raise, confront registered nurses many times in their careers, sometimes on a daily basis. In most nursing schools, however, there is not one required philosophy course until the doctoral level!

And, it is a rare course that ever mentions the power and efficacy of political action. Except for an occasional classroom "guest" who urges the student nurse to join a professional organization or to sign a petition, there is no mention of one of society's most dynamic means of effecting change — the political process.

To be sure, nurses are introduced to the lofty precepts which touch upon the subjects of feminism, business, law, philosophy, marketing, and politics, but, for the most part, this introduction is theoretical. When a random nursing student actually puts theory into action, s/he is rarely supported by either her peers or the educators who have propounded them. Rather, she is considered somewhat of a rebellious curiosity, more valued as an amusing iconoclast than as a paradigm or inspiration. This is all the more regrettable in light of the modern nurse's excellent preparedness in other areas. While she is ill-equipped to serve her own best needs, she is superbly equipped to serve the patients'.

The registered nurse of the '80s had, at minimum, a three-year hospital diploma degree. Many had associate degrees which included a two-year, supervised clinical experience. Increasingly, nurses have either Bachelor's or Master's degrees which include studies in the social sciences, biochemistry, physics, microbiology, statistics, physiology, biology, and pharmacology — and also in the vital aspects of daily patient care. These nurses must have a sophisticated knowledge of monitoring, suctioning, dialyzing and intravenous devices and routines, and also in-depth knowledge of the great variety of modern medications, their actions and untoward reactions, and of intervention protocols.

And, because so many patients are now discharged from hospitals in serious condition, the modern home-health nurse, away from the "protective" environment of the hospital, must embody an even greater degree of independent judgment. In addition, nurses must carry malpractice insurance, which places culpability for patient care solely in their domain. Today, many nurses practice independently as psychotherapists, midwives, pediatric and family practitioners, and advanced nurse practitioners. Others are university administrators and professors, community liaisons, the list goes on.

Several persuasive studies have shown that nurses who share power (i.e. decision-making, nursing diagnoses, administrative input, control over their own budgets) have greater job longevity and satisfaction than those who are employed and exploited by places that do not demonstrate a similar respect. While wages are, indeed, a major issue, it is clearly not the arch criterion by which nurses judge the value of their jobs. Even when salaries increase, grievances persist.

Certainly, the pernicious sexist hangover that characterizes administrative intransigence accounts for some of the dissatisfaction. However, many of nursing's problems are the result of the contradictory and self-abnegating lessons which have been foisted upon generations of nursing students: "Yes, you're valuable, but don't tell anyone, you might alienate them." "Yes, you deserve more pay, but don't demand it, you might lost your job." "Yes, you have a superior body of knowledge and legal accountability, but don't make waves, you're dispensable." These destructive messages, in conjunction with a uniformly inadequate curriculum, conspire to put all nurses at a disadvantage" (Swirsky, 1988).

Solution #1: Academia

Nurses are more than the sum of their parts   more than their choice of career, clinical function, and specialty area. Nursing education must introduce this concept to nurses on more than a didactic level. For instance, it always struck me as odd that, at the beginning of each semester, when and if nurses are asked to introduce themselves to their classmates, they are never expected (or encouraged) to include anything personal about themselves. In over 17 years of sitting in nursing classrooms, I rarely heard a nurse introduce herself (or himself) with more than a just-the-facts-ma'am laundry list: "My name is Jane Smith," a typical introduction would begin. "I work at Queens General Hospital in the emergency department. Before that, I worked at Stony Brook Hospital in the intensive-care unit. Someday, I'd like to go into administration."

What, I wonder, does this person do in her leisure time. What outside interests does she have? What kind of music does she like? Is she involved in any volunteer activities? Is she political? Artistic? Mechanical? A skydiver? Does she have children? If so, how many: four? nine? If these and other facets of her life were elicited, if she were given the impression that they really do define her more fully, then perhaps she would be encouraged to implement the qualities she brings to other pursuits to the pursuit of nursing.

For example: she might bring the courage of skydiving to negotiations with administrators, the love of music to her patient's bedside, the volunteer impulse to that "extra" gesture, the skill at juggling domesticity with academia and nursing to administrative tasks. Too often, concepts taught in the classroom are learned but not incorporated. When they are personalized, they become more "real," and thus more applicable. If nursing faculties made it their business to learn more of the vital living experiences of their nursing students, they would be able to affirm to them that their personal frames of reference and the lessons they had learned have value, the kind of value they might take into the clinical setting.

In addition, nursing curricula must be revolutionized to include subjects (again, such as feminism, business, ethics, etc.) that have direct relevance to the nursing experience. But where, one may ask, will "the experts" in fields like business, law, feminist thought, philosophy, politics come from? Simply, from other institutions or from the public sector where they exist. Why must nursing schools, unlike other centers of higher learning, rely exclusively on their existing faculty or draw only from their own ranks or from an occasional lecturer from the "outside" world? There is a vast wealth of resource people willing and able to impart their expertise. Nursing schools must find these people and utilize them wisely if nurses of the future are to be equipped, in all areas, for the jobs they will perform.

But, what of the courses that already exist? In the case of many, get rid of them! Nowhere can more "dead wood" be found than in current nursing curricula. Nursing schools must stop teaching small-group process, problem-solving techniques, assertiveness training, and all the other narcotizing courses that teach nurses more how to "behave" than how to prevail.

There must also be a better system of evaluating faculty. There is not a nurse who cannot recount a tale of at least one teacher who was ignorant, uninformed, punitive, competitive with her students, intolerant, lazy, or terminally boring. Yet, in spite of mandatory evaluations at the end of each semester, the same teachers continues to contaminate the classroom with their inferior teaching or their mean-spiritedness, and they continue to waste the valuable time of nursing students, many of whom hold full-time jobs and/or raise families.

What do nursing-school administrators do with these evaluations? Do they visit the classrooms to evaluate for themselves the truthfulness of the evaluations? Do they suggest relevant courses (in, for instance, human relations) or recommend psychotherapy to teachers who are so evaluated, the better for them to alter their behavior? Do they review the tenure system to find ways to relieve such teachers from their classroom tyranny? These strategies are infrequently, if ever, employed. These kinds of teachers, like death and taxes, are always there. But, need they be? I think not. Here, too, action is imperative if the seeds of NURSE ABUSE are to be eradicated.

In terms of required texts, it is important to mention that many "authoritative" sources continue to employ gender-biased language. When a nursing student reads that "man believes" ("thinks," "feels," "postulates," etc.), or any other statements that imply that action and thought almost unilaterally derive from the male of the species, there is the very real feeling that what s/he has read precludes, not only 100 percent of most nursing classes, but 97 percent of the nursing profession as well.

While some modern texts are written or edited with a sensitivity to the universality of most experiences, most continue to be riddled with statements that both assert and imply the primacy of male thought and experience. The subtle, yet powerful, message this kind of language conveys cannot be calculated in terms of the demoralizing effects it has on the female nursing student it clearly does not address. It behooves nursing instructors to be sensitive to this issue and to seek out those texts which do not reflect such flagrant and destructive gender bias.

Problem #2: Politics

As nursing has evolved since the early 1900s in America, it has gone from a profession characterized by servility, self-abnegation, obedience, passivity, and dependence to one which at least strives to be more active, assertive, self-defining, and independent. Even now, however, in the 1990s, after literally decades of social ferment and revolutions both economic and sexual, nurses do not wield the "clout" that other, more aggressive constituencies have acquired in our political system.

Political action is not new to nursing. Early nurses, such as Lillian Wald, Lavinia Dock, et al., were politically involved, and nurses since that time have attempted with some measure of success to affect important changes through political action.

With the advent of Nurses for Political Action in 1971, and its absorption into the ANA's N-CAP (Nurses Coalition for Political Action), nurses began to have some power, however limited, in public policies that affected their professional lives. The Nurse Training Act of 1971, among others, took on the responsibility of enforcing provisions of laws that prohibited sex discrimination.

Even before that, the feminist revolution of the 1960s brought about several important changes. The institution of NOW (National Organization for Women) spearheaded long-overdue legislative change for the betterment of women. Using Title VII of the 1964 Civil Rights Act, which prohibited economic discrimination on the basis of sex, NOW and other organizations worked effectively to tear down ancient barriers that excluded women from equal access to good jobs.

Over the last decade, a significant increase in independent nurse practitioners has enlarged the pool of political nurse activists who have fought for legislation necessary for them to survive and flourish independently. There have been a spate of lawsuits focusing on academic grievances and workplace inequities. And a growing number of nurses (including students) have plunged into the political process.

Organizations have proliferated, rules and regulations have been formulated, and, indeed, some important legislation *has* been passed. A greater number of nurses are now participating in the political process, be they as members of professional organizations, "grass roots" coalitions, lobbyists, or organizers. If one is looking for examples of greater participation, they can be found. However, considering there are over two-million registered nurses in this country, the vast potential of nursing as a political force has yet to be realized. It is certainly safe to say that nurses are gravely underrepresented in the political life of our nation.

It may be that the kinds of people nursing attracts are, by nature, apolitical, more attuned to giving than taking, more comfortable with meeting the needs of others than expecting or demanding that their own needs be met. Perhaps, it is their perception of themselves as essentially powerless that prevents many nurses from seeking solutions to their problems in the political arena in which the assertion of power is a given.

People who are politically active almost consistently entertain the notion that they, personally, can *do* something to make a difference. They believe that through *their* vote, *their* participation, and *their* involvement, they can effect (and affect) change. Intrinsically political issues, such as war and peace, crime, health reform, hiring-and-firing policies, or equity in pay, are all larger than the individual who faces them on a daily basis. It is only through political action that these issues can be addressed in any meaningful way, precisely because it is only through our legislators (and the legislation they either do or do not enact) that both our needs and desires can be met.

Although there have always been notable examples of nurses

who have appreciated the power of political action and were involved in such action themselves, by and large nurses have been apolitical. Why is it that the clear cause-and-effect lessons that political life demonstrates has been so long in reaching nursing consciousness?

For many years, the ranks of nurses came from women who, while aspiring to some sense of identity outside of the home, were attracted to work that was largely perceived as extra-domestic: nurturing, care-taking, and subordinate to authority. Even in the 1970s, the choice of nursing as a career did not include the search for an education which went beyond the bounds of "training." With the reevaluation of nursing curricula and the subsequent suggestion to standardize entry-level requirements to include a Baccalaureate degree, a "new" kind of nurse was envisioned, one whose education would include at least a dabbling in the humanities, the social sciences, history, and philosophy.

This re-evaluation coincided with the feminist revolution and the sweeping changes it brought to the structure of our society. As female-male relationships underwent a virtual metamorphosis, as more than 50 percent of women entered the work force, and as medical technology exploded in a proliferation of new treatments, machines, expectations, and responsibilities, the decision of nurses to place themselves in the context of modern society came not one minute too soon.

Before then, the education of nurses was tailor-made to fulfil the roles they were expected to execute as auxiliary health-care providers and the passive recipients of others' orders and directives. It is no wonder that, up until the last decade, most nurses (again, to be sure, with notable exceptions) had a limited awareness of the power of political action.

One reason, perhaps the major reason, why nurses' participation in political life has been so inadequate is because schools of nursing have never taught their students that political strategies, both within and outside of the hospital, could be utilized effectively to address their grievances. Wiping their hands of political action, nursing educators dismiss their students into the hostile and highly political hospital environment, leaving their political education up to state and national nursing organizations. But it is a classic case of "too little, too late." By the time nurses enter their careers, they are already in a lion's den, surrounded by carnivores and pitifully unequipped to fight their own battles.

In most institutions, nurses are taught to address their grievances to the nursing supervisor or head nurse, their putative allies. But these "allies" are not allies at all. In fact, they have been subsumed by Machiavellian administrations that have figured out exactly how *not* to share power. The age-old ploy goes like this: administration selects not only talented, but potentially "trouble-making" nurses for promotion, making their rewards higher salary, prestigious title, and increased status that are irresistibly attractive to nurses who have had none of these goodies. Within seconds of such a promotion, these nurses become de facto members of administration and, de facto, adversaries and not allies of their staff-nurse colleagues.

In an all-too-typical scenario, the nurse who needs an advocate or who wants to resolve a problem goes to his or her supervisor or head nurse. Instead of the ally s/he expects, s/he finds delaying tactics, endless meetings, or stone-walling. A "can't-fight-City-Hall" mentality develops as the nurse's anger and frustration are met with lip service, patronizing inattention, or the kind of irritation usually reserved for buzzing gnats.

Conditioned to believe they are essentially powerless, it rarely occurs to staff nurses in this kind of position to address their grievances to the Board of Trustees, or write an exposé in a local newspaper, or lodge a lawsuit against the institution. After these kinds of experiences, it is fruitless to talk to nurses of the "power" political action can yield. Power feels good. But like any other asset, it only feels good to the person who recognizes it exists. It is as meaningless to tell a beautiful girl who thinks of herself as ugly to get a modeling job as it is to tell a nurse who feels powerless to exercise her power.

Nursing perpetuates this sense of powerlessness by asking the wrong questions. While we debate amongst ourselves whether or not nursing is, indeed, a profession, are we not straining at a flea and swallowing an elephant? If we do not enjoy the privileges of professionalism, is the debate relevant? In the same sense, is it important for nursing to ask what job titles afford the most prestige, if all job titles are essentially powerless in the hospital hierarchy? And, yet again, is it crucial for nursing educators to ask for increased science courses in their curricula if nurses are not considered equal partners in the prevailing health-care system and called upon to share and practice what they've learned?

In the experience of most nurses, exercising clinical expertise and judgment is curtailed by a complex system of medical, legal and institutional restraints. While nursing observation, for instance, may denote that a particular regimen is indicated or a combination of medications is having an untoward effect, the nurse cannot implement independent action but is compelled to pass his or her observations to a variety of medical specialists who then act on the advice to the benefit of the patient. Of course, it is *they* who receive the positive feedback (if not downright adulation), and the nurse who is left in the background, while others take action. How can nurses think of themselves as powerful if even the real power they have is appropriated from them?

Is this bleak picture a blueprint for the future of nursing? Too many hopeful possibilities exist to draw that conclusion.

Solution #2: Politics

In nursing schools and in the workplace, the subject of politics must be made a central issue, introduced as the vehicle through which major changes can be made. Once the structure and function of government and institutions are understood, nursing issues must be placed on the "front burner." Are independent nurse practitioners allowed third-party payment privileges in my state? Where is the resistance from the medical community? The insurance companies? Are non-professionals or paraprofessionals allowed to perform nursing functions, in spite of their non-licensure? Are hospitals violating union agreements with impunity? The list of political issues, as they affect nursing, goes on. In order to address them politically, they must first be known.

Both nursing schools and hospital nursing administrations should offer credits or CEU's for the nurse who mobilizes a constituency; in politics, there is strength in numbers. Nurses with political experience should teach mini-workshops to demonstrate the actual 'how-to' of political action: letter-writing campaigns, lobbying, phone calls and visits to local legislators, media advertising, fund-raising, and, most important, voter-registration drives to mobilize sympathetic constituencies. It is truly amazing how attentive politicians are to those blocs which express their most fervent desires in the voting booth.

In a political-action organization to which I belong, candidates are interviewed personally (at the homes of members of the organization) and queried as to where they stand on the issues most central to the organization's philosophy — in our view, there are right answers and wrong answers. We take the opportunity to educate the politicians in the event their answers are either misguided or antagonistic.

In just a few short years, we have found the politicians using us as resource people and utilizing our endorsements in their advertising campaigns. It matters to them that we vote! And, because of our interviewing and endorsement policy, letter-writing and phone call activity, and the numbers of people who are sympathetic to our philosophy (all of whom also vote), we find their responsiveness increasing significantly each year.

The political process is available to all people. But, like all processes, it needs to be learned and then implemented. When nursing enters the political mainstream and becomes a force that demands recognition, nursing issues will earn the responsiveness they deserve. And, when the principles of political action are applied in the work setting, progress will be made.

Problem #3: Feminism

Throughout history, women have worked in outside-of-the-home jobs. In this country, even before they pursued the "traditional" jobs of teacher, nurse, and secretary, women worked in "mom-and-pop" enterprises, at home in "cottage industries," in sweat shops, in mills, and in fields. In 1900, almost all women workers served as domestics, farm laborers, unskilled factory operatives, or teachers. Yet, by 1920, in spite of the suffrage movement, traditional attitudes remained fixed, jobs remained segregated according to gender, and women's jobs were defined as "woman's work."

The economic and social history of women in this country is also the history of nurses. However, because nurses were among the first to enter the labor force, their grievances are particularly galling. Throughout the decades of the 20th Century, nurses have been heiresses to all of the biases, wage discrimination, and sexist thinking and acting that has plagued the larger population of women as well.

Within four years from the start of World War II, more than six-million women entered the job market in response to an unprecedented demand for new workers and new production. At the time, the government, in support of the need for female workers to compensate for the men away at war, allocated $6 million dollars for war nursery schools. When the war was over in 1945, many women chose to remain in the work force, so beginning our current system of the two-wage family.

Many of the women who chose to work outside of the home did so only when their children were of school age. In addition, because our society was less mobile, working women could frequently count on family members or trusted neighbors to care for their children. Also, the one-parent family, a by-product of the divorce mania that was to sweep the country, was then a relatively rare phenomenon. It would not be long before divorced women would enter the work force out of the sheer necessity to insure that both they and their children survived.

During the 1950s, twice as many women were on the job as in 1940. However, even as more women were pursuing professions once held to be the exclusive domain of men, society-at-large was keeping women in their traditionally devalued place. The disparity in pay scales remained wide and opportunities for advancement remained enduring obstacles.

In 1960 came The Pill, the feminist movement, and the sexual revolution. With the advent of the birth-control pill, women forsook early marriage in order to explore the increasing variety of opportunities that loomed on the horizon of a changing society. The feminist movement fueled these efforts, reminding women that, by controlling their own biological destinies, they could concentrate on other facets of their development. As the feminist movement took hold, "traditional" roles were called into question on all fronts, economic as well as domestic.

Many women were deferring marriage and motherhood in pursuit of a career. Some found themselves in satisfying careers, many of which demanded great responsibility and an obeisance to "the rules of the game," namely, no children. Those who chose to have children found they were living in the only industrial nation in the world that had no national system of parental leave. With increasing economic independence, women who had once languished in bad marriages (or in non-marital relationships), left them.

As the divorce rate rose (to one out of two marriages), so did the standard of living. Married women, many out of economic necessity, others to attain satisfying careers, became part of a family complex in which two salaries were required to fulfil a viable standard of living. Many divorced women found themselves on the receiving end of flouted child-support payments and with no means of supporting their families other than joining the work force.

During the 1970s, the two-family income had become a common phenomenon. Yet, through all this change, some things remained the same. The vast majority of women continued to work in sex-segregated occupations, concentrating in service industries, female clerical jobs, government positions, teaching, and nursing. Also, women continued to be denied access to decision-making and executive positions and to have job-related necessities (such as maternity leave or day care) addressed with any degree of support or seriousness.

Now, in the '90s, with increasing numbers of women entering the work force and becoming mothers, many of the old inequities have still not been effectively addressed. In the vital areas of pay equity and advancement opportunities, progress has been sluggish. In the area of day care, problems of inadequate legislation, meager funding, poor regulation, and underpaid staff workers abound. In addition, concerns about the psychological effects of day care on children less than one year of age, on toddlers, on older children, and on the mothers who must juggle parental and economic responsibilities all are in question.

According to Edward Zigler, Director of Yale University's Bush Center in Child Development and Social Policy, three-quarters of the nation's working women have school-age children; half have infants less than a year old. Yet, in spite of the radical changes society has undergone in the past three decades, all the issues that plagued women in the 1960s are alive and well in the 1990s, with some of them, such as the intransigence of male "role" behavior, having become more exaggerated and infuriating with time.

The 1990s has brought little change in the demands placed on women in the workplace, and little change in terms of their compensation. Called the "decade of corporate greed," the past several years have seen corporation CEOs and shareholders push their profits through the roof by eliminating as many employees as is possible. Health-care has been no exception. The job security that nurses once knew, flawed as it was, is no more. The benefits hospitals once offered their staffs are being eliminated.

In spite of a recently passed Parental Leave Act, women are still without on-site day care for their children and, worse, are still subject to losing their jobs if they leave to have children. Currently, job-protected, paid maternity leaves, most of them very brief, are available to fewer than 40 percent of employed mothers. Groups such as the National Federation of Independent Businesses and the National Association of Manufacturers oppose parental leave, citing issues of cost and the threat to employee relationships. Given these circumstances, it is not surprising that a Census Bureau report (May, 1988) said that the inability to find a babysitter disrupted the jobs of 450,000 women nationally each month.

According to economist Sylvia Ann Hewlett (1986, p. 97), "Women are joining the European work force at much the same rate and for much the same reasons as in America. But there is one major difference. In Europe, working women are supported by an elaborate (and in most cases expanding) family-support system, which is a major factor behind their improved earning power. It is no coincidence that the country with the most developed benefits and services for working women, Sweden, is also the country with the smallest wage gap, while the country with the least developed benefits and services, the United States, is also the country with one of the largest wage gaps."

In spite of some grand protestations to the contrary, it is clear that the oldest and most destructive stereotypes about women and about the task of caring for children have not significantly improved. "Woman's work" has, for the most part, been considered primarily that of childbearer and childrearer. Historically devalued, these roles have also been perceived by some women, at least those who agree with their detractors' definition of worth, as intrinsically less valuable than those of wage earners.

Now, as more and more women pursue the male-defined characterization of success — the salary — they find that society is wildly out of sync with their most cherished fantasies about how they will be perceived. Rather than the heightened esteem they have been led to believe accrues to those who "earn a buck," women are finding that neither they nor their job status have resulted in more esteem from employers. Nurses know this as well as, if not better, than the rest of the female working force in America. Is this issue too big for the nurses of our country to handle? Decidedly not.

Solution #3: Feminism

Roots! Women must learn from whence they came in order to know in which direction they want to go and in order to appreciate the formidable historical, social, cultural, and psychological obstacles that stand in their way. In the case of nurses, it is incumbent upon every nursing school to incorporate into its curriculum courses on feminism: feminist thought, philosophy, history. It is important for nurses to understand how being women has affected every facet of their lives, from the Bible to the ERA, from the first flicker of the Nightingale lamp to the last check an R.N. made out for malpractice insurance.

If Carol Gilligan (1982, p. 160) is correct (and I believe she is) when she says that "...the female comes to know herself as she is known, through her relationships with others...." then it is clear that when the nurse is devalued (abused!) in the workplace and in society in general, she comes to devalue herself. Conversely, if nurses re-evaluate themselves in positive terms — and on their own terms — their self-images will be immeasurably enhanced, both personally and professionally.

On an individual level, nurses can form "consciousness-raising" groups, forums in which experiences are exchanged, common problems are discussed, solutions and strategies are formulated, and support is shared.

Feminist literature can be invigorating and illuminating, broadening the perspective and shedding light on the common denominators of the female experience.

And feminist organizations, such as the National Organization of Women (which has local chapters in most cities) and the National Women's Health Network (to name but two) can be valuable resources and support agencies, as well as avenues of action and participation.

One of the most positive aspects of feminist thinking is the pride is engenders in being a female, in valuing those unequaled qualities which are so unique to the female experience. Michael Polanyi (1958, p. 53) said that "It is pathetic to watch the endless efforts equipped with microscopy and chemistry, with mathematics and electronics to reproduce a single violin of the kind the half-literate Stradivarius turned out as a matter of routine more than 200 years ago."

Of course, the nurse is not a half-literate creature. However, in the "art" of her nursing role, she can proudly turn to those feminine qualities that have for so long and with such inaccuracy been demeaned: the ability to relate, to give, to be compassionate, the capacity for empathy, the talent for nurturing. What better way to humanize "modern medicine"?

If political action is a power of one kind, then valuing oneself as a woman is a power of another kind. Feminism teaches this. Nursing must begin to consider the "feminine" aspect of the profession in a positive way and nurses must predicate their theories and actions, their very raison d'être, on the feminine principle.

Problem #4: Advertising & Marketing

I remember hearing a story about "the greatest advertising coup in history." An advertising firm was hired to market Alka Seltzer and one of their clever jingle writers composed a tune to which the words, "Plop, plop, fizz, fizz, oh what a relief it is," were sung. Anticipated sales doubled and, to this day, continue to be twice what they might have been because the public was led to believe that, in order to get the "relief" they sought, they had to take *two* Alka Seltzers ("plop, plop") instead of the one tablet that would have done the trick! How amazing! The ability to sell people something — even something they don't need! — just with an inventive and catchy sales approach!

Of course, our entire economy is fueled by advertising and marketing. Billions are spent on cosmetics, largely the function of the "creative" ability of Madison Avenue admen to convince women that they need this or that product in order to be attractive, desirable, sexy, or just plain acceptable. Mail-order catalogues generate huge sales selling people items (and many times gimmicks) they could live an entire lifetime without. Certainly, advertising also serves to illuminate people about the things they really do need. The sales of everything from cars to appliances to homes to leisure gear to reading material, ad infinitum — all depend upon advertising and marketing.

In today's world, universities advertise their virtues, physician ads fill up the Yellow Pages, and hospitals take full-page advertisements to lure potential clients. Now that the rest of the professional world has caught on to the power of advertising and marketing, a proliferation of ads featuring accounting firms, chiropractic and dentistry practices, and law services fill the air waves and television screen and occupy a good deal of space in the print media.

However, the advertising and marketing of nurses is nowhere to be found. To be sure, nurses have independent practices in midwifery, in psychotherapy, as clinical nurse specialists in a variety of areas. They have skills in management, in community liaison work, in teaching. They conduct seminars and CPR classes and join life-saving units. But, because they don't "go public," the public's "image" of nurses remains fixated in the past or wedded to the current images that movies and television portray.

In these depictions, the nurse is either toting a bed-pan, shaking down a thermometer, jumping into bed with an eager patient, the embodiment of wicked Nurse Ratchet, the machinating plotter on a soap opera or TV show, or the seductive, hare-brained floozy portrayed on greeting cards.

Where is the nurse who imparts information, who reacts coolly and effectively in an emergency, who teaches pre-operative patients, who delivers a baby, who diagnoses and treats a depressed patient, who lobbies a state senator, who runs a critical-care unit, who performs bedside nursing of the highest order, who assists in complicated surgery or diagnostic procedures, who saves a life?

We know s/he is there. We are these nurses! What to do?

Solution #4: Advertising and Marketing

Nurses must put their own best foot forward. I remember a conversation I had just after becoming a certified childbirth instructor in 1979. When the subject of how to attract clients arose, it was clear that the consensus of the people I was speaking with thought that advertising was "unprofessional." Since their arguments were not convincing, I decided to embark on what Norman Mailer called "Advertisements for Myself." Although I had stopped working in the delivery room, I wrote a letter, not only to the doctors I had worked with, but to doctors I had never met whose names I found in the phone book.

In the letter, I cited my delivery-room experience, my accreditation in a nationally recognized childbirth association, a brief synopsis of the course I would be teaching, the geographical convenience of my home (where I teach) to their offices, the advantages of the small-size classes I would be teaching, and some personal attributes I thought might appeal to them.

The return I got was about four-to-five percent, less than I had anticipated, but creditable according to the business people with whom I spoke. However, that one mailing put me "on the map" and allowed the word-of-mouth "buzz" that is so vital to any business enterprise to happen more quickly than if I had not advertised. In addition, I hung advertisements in local supermarkets and spoke at local forums.

In no time, it seemed, my practice began to flourish and, as a bonus, I became a resource person (sometimes voluntary, sometimes in a paid capacity) to both nurses and other women and men who wanted to establish independent enterprises. Then, as now, I could not see how the advertising and marketing I did for myself is or was in any way unprofessional. In fact, everyone involved benefitted from my efforts: my clients, the doctors, the people I advised, and me.

I have known other nurses who, catching the entrepreneurial spirit, have parlayed their background in nursing into profitable ventures. One runs a CPR company, teaching large corporations the techniques of cardiopulmonary resuscitation. Another runs workshops in various industries, teaching techniques for better communication and stress reduction. Another started a business doing check-ups and health teaching for insurance companies. Another started a private day-care center. And, yet another started a holistic health-care practice. All of these nurses advertised and marketed themselves aggressively, using their nursing backgrounds to establish their credentials, credibility, and authority.

Unfortunately, however, the actions of a few do not speak for the many. Nurses, especially now when our profession's very lifeblood is being threatened, must institute a national advertising campaign that tells the American public who we are, what we do, and how vital our contribution to the American health-care system is. On an individual level, nurses should take every opportunity to tout themselves, to let the public-at-large know that we feel dignity in our choice of career, that we know our own worth, and that we won't be undersold!

Problem #5: Business & Law

When nurses go into a hospital, they find themselves in the middle of a business enterprise with few, if any, business skills. They are called upon a punch a time clock, adhere to "company" regulations, deal with "higher-ups," and execute their jobs without "making waves." Often, they find themselves in the middle of questionable practices (i.e. mandatory overtime, understaffing, harassment, general NURSE ABUSE.)

Finding themselves in unequitable positions, it is difficult for nurses to challenge existing policies or defend themselves if they don't know how the hospital business works or they don't have at least a rudimentary familiarity with the law. Does it have to be this way? Absolutely not.

Solution #5: Business & Law

Nursing schools should encourage nurses (for credit) to do field work in the business and law setting. Even a half semester of such experience would familiarize the nurse with the internal workings of those respective settings, equip him or her with the beginning tools to deal with the kinds of problems s/he will encounter in the hospital.

In the hospital, nurses must insist that they be invited to seminars and meetings which focus upon these subjects. They must take advantage of the many seminars given in their communities and around the country which directly address the business and/or legal issues that confront them. Many of these seminars are given by nurses for nurses; many are given by people from the business and law community.

The purpose of gathering this type of information is empowerment. It is not only that knowledge diminishes the anxiety that arises when people find themselves in unfamiliar or threatening situations, it is also that knowledge endows people with a sense of their own authority, a sense that they are not victims but full participants in the events of their lives.

Problem #6: Psychology

The Talmud says: "We do not see things the way they are. We see things the way we are." Because our view of the world is limited to our own perspective and our own experience, it is easy to see how a person who has been devalued comes to devalue himself or herself. S/he will see things through the jaded prism of his or her own vision and not "as they are." In the same way, a person whose life experience has been fraught with anger and disappointment will see the world, not as a benevolent and caring place, but as one which holds potential threats. Even in the absence of evidence, that person will see things, not as they are, but as s/he is. Ultimately, the best chance we all have to change the things in our lives that displease us is to change ourselves.

I once attended a seminar in which the moderator explained that there were only three ways that people truly change: through a close brush with death, through a profoundly religious experience, or through psychotherapy. I cannot attest to the validity of this theory, but I do believe that people who *want* to change *can* change.

Of course, it would be ideal if children were not raised in sexist environments or in settings which devalue females. It would also be wonderful if females and males could be perceived according to who they were, and not according to the still rigid "gender roles" which determine so much of modern life. However, before these global changes come to pass, the best we can do is to be aware of our own implication in the lives we lead and to strive for the kinds of personal and societal changes we desire.

Solution #6: Psychology

For those contemplating psychotherapy, there are several schools which might be considered:

Psychotherapy:

> Sometimes called psychodynamic psychotherapy, this
> method attributes emotional problems to unconscious

internal conflicts. It is usually a lengthy process (for which modern insurance companies resist co-payments) in which childhood traumas are explored, dreams analyzed, and transference phenomena given important interpretive meaning. Psychotherapy explores symptoms by identifying the pattern of defense and the developmental history of the symptoms. In this type of psychotherapy, change is usually slower in coming than in some other types of therapy. It is for the patient who is highly motivated to change and who is interested in learning of the symbolic nature of her or his symptoms.

Cognitive Therapy:

This treatment focuses on altering troublesome thoughts. Developed by Aaron Beck, a psychiatrist at the University of Pennsylvania, it is predicated on the theory that the ways in which we think about ourselves and the world affect how we feel and behave. When the therapist points out to the patient his or her cognitive errors and then teaches methods in rethinking, both feelings and behavior are altered.

Behavioral Therapy:

Based on Pavlovian conditioning, this therapy operates on the premise that behavior is affected by either positive or negative reinforcement. The goal is to get patients to learn new and more appropriate responses. This type of therapy is particularly effective in treat-

ing phobias and other behavioral problems that inter-
fere with normal daily living.

Interpersonal Therapy:

This therapy attributes psychological problems to
faulty relationships. Frequently, it includes family
members who, through the therapeutic milieu, learn
in which ways their behavior influences the existing
problem.

These are but a few of the myriad of types of therapies that
exist. In addition, there are group therapies, support groups, psycho-
drama (in which emotional situations are acted out), consciousness-
raising groups, and crisis-intervention therapy, again, to name but a
few.

But that is not to omit the "therapy" that people can give to
themselves. Sometimes, all it take is a deep conversation with an
empathic person or reading a book that is particularly inspiring to
bring about important changes in one's life.

And so, when it comes to "Solutions," there are an abun-
dance of possibilities, ranging from the personal to the legal to the
political to the academic to the psychological. For the nurse who
feels that she "can't take it anymore" and is tired of the NURSE
ABUSE that pervades her life, these may offer a good start at changing those things which can be changed.

The current crisis in nursing — indeed, the future of nursing
itself — can be resolved only if we invoke the "Nurse - Heal Thyself" philosophy. It is time to turn our full attention, not to the image
we have had, but to the substance that we have. Nursing must take a
hard and critical look at itself, acknowledge its flaws, and then embark on revolutionary measures of change.

References

Brown, S. A. (1985). Perspective on Why Nurses Should Earn Doctorates in Nursing. *Perspectives in Psychiatric Care.* 23(1).

Corea, G. (1977). *The Hidden Malpractice: How American Medicine Treats Women as Patients and Professionals.* New York: William Morrow & Company.

Dentzer, S. (1988). Calling The shots In Health Care: The Nursing Shortage Points Up A Growing Turf War Between Doctors and Nurses. *U.S. News and World Report,* July, 11.

Ehrenreich, B., & English, D. (1973). *Witches, Midwives and Nurses.* New York: The Feminist Press.

Gilligan, C. (1982). *In A Different Voice: Psychological Theory and Women's Development.* Cambridge: Harvard University Press.

Hewlett, S. A. (1986). *A Lesser Life: The Myth of Women's Liberation in America.* New York: Warner Books.

Kuhn, T. S. (1970). *The Structure of Scientific Revolutions.* Chicago: University of Chicago Press.

Polanyi, M. (1958). *Personal Knowledge.* Chicago: University of Chicago Press.

Riehl, J. P. & Callista, R. (1980). *Conceptual Model for Nursing Practice.* Norwalk, Connecticut: Appleton-Century-Crofts.

Swirsky, J. (1988). Nurse - Heal Thyself. *The New York Times.* May 22.

Chapter Eight

NURSES BILL OF RIGHTS

by Laura Gasparis Vonfrolio, RN, Ph.D., CEN, CCRN
Donna Shea Leear, R.N., B.S.N., CCRN
Theresa Mastrorilli, R.N., B.S.N., CCRN

1.   *Registered nurses warrant fair and equitable com-*
     pensation as is given to other professionals with com
     parable education, expertise, and responsibility.

2.   *It is nursing's privilege to consider and implement*
     collective bargaining in order to secure and resolve
     the issue of comparable worth.

3.   *Nurses have a right to receive direct reimbursement*
     in the form of fee-for-service for the comprehensive
     and skilled care they provide.

4.   *Nurses must have the right to refuse reassignment to*
     patient-care areas foreign to their area of speciality
     practice, for nurses must be regarded as unique prac-
     titioners, not interchangeable commodities.

5. *Nurses must be respected and valued by colleagues as integral and vital members of the healthcare team, their assessments and recommendations considered essential in formulating the strategies of patient care.*

6. *Nurses employed in a bureaucratic institution are entitled to the respect and support of that institution's administration regarding issues concerned with the delivery of patient care.*

7. *Nurses must be able to participate actively in formulating policies that directly affect them and their patients.*

8. *Employers are obligated to establish an environment in which nurses are actively involved in determining the standards of practice necessary for implementing quality patient care.*

9. *Employers must provide adequate ancillary services to abolish time spent by nurses with non-nursing duties.*

10. *Nurses must be guaranteed a technologically efficient environment in which to function, enabling them to maximize the time required to deliver direct patient care.*

11. *Financial support must be available to nurses for the enhancement of clinical knowledge and attainment of educational goals.*

12. *An effective mechanism of disciplinary action must be established in which nurses, as patient advocates, may report professional incompetence and situations that compromise patient care.*